Para ab normal in Kentucky

Para ab normal in Kentucky

A COLLECTION OF TRUE STORIES

Diane Satterfield

ISBN-13: 9780692929407
ISBN-10: 0692929401

Dedicated with love to My Children,
Christopher: "it might have appeared to go unnoticed, but I've got it all here in my heart....I would be nothing without you.1
Jessica: a heart that is forever determined, sometimes fragile, and always true.
Heather: an angel with a wistful sigh; the only little rabbit I can catch.

*I have written my book, not in chronological years,
but in spiritual footsteps.*

Table of Contents

I am amazed at how our very ordinary world can be turned upside down when a parade of the bizarre and paranormal decides to befriend, or torment us. Life can become disturbing, and we become wary, because we don't always know what is on the other side of the door. Sometimes we don't answer, but they come in anyway. They can be familiar, strangers, or the unknown. They may be the ones who love us, and want to protect us, but they may not be. And sometimes Heaven steps in to save us.

"Introduction; Why Para *ab* normal in Kentucky"

—∞—

I STARTED WRITING THIS BOOK because my children wanted me to record the extraordinary, and sometimes bizarre events that have become a real part of our world. I thought that it might be interesting reading for future family generations who might wonder what their ancestors did for fun, or excitement, or to make their hair stand up on end. However, I came to realize that it might serve another purpose as well.

I have always wondered why the things that happened, happened to us. In the eyes of the world, we are not extraordinary by any means. Personally, I have had more failures than I can count, and seemingly misunderstood or acted too late to take advantage of opportunities hand over fist; multi-chances that have made my heart sink when I realized what I had done, or lost.

I hope this book will help others like me who have struggled to realize that all is not lost or in vain; that if miracles can happen to me, they can happen to anyone. I came to understand that life may be filled with amazing, sometimes unexplainable things, and if we don't necessarily feel amazing or extraordinary, we still are, and we matter. Perhaps that is why these things happened, and why I feel compelled to share them with you.

I have asked God into my heart, only to make choices in my life that were not only devastating to me, but to my children. I feel that I not only failed myself and my family over and over, but God as well. I lived in deep faith, only to sink to the depths of despair and disbelief. I've been angry, sorry, and ignorant of God's love; repentant, and through it all again.

Mine has been a life of plenty, and want, and back around. Not just once, but many times. I've been up, and I've been down, and every time I really believed that this was it, that God had really had it with this stubborn, weak-willed, and pathetic creature, some wonderful thing would happen. Not just wonderful, but miraculous.

I came to realize that these true and personal accounts might encourage, and perhaps rekindle the faith of those that have had their ups and downs in life, just as I have. Be assured that God is not only still with you, but He never left, and what's more, He never will.

I would say that my life has never been what you could call "normal and status quo." I desired a safe and secure home for my family, and the happiness that an ordinary and comfortable life in mid-America could offer; but it was not to be. From where I started, and where I have found myself throughout the years is a long way from that Disney fairy-tale.

The love and humor that my children and I shared, among tears, may have been our saving grace, but it did not spare us from the abnormal, the unknown, and the sometimes incomprehensible. But with that, as the years have passed along, we are realizing that we are part of an even greater saving grace than we can imagine.

If there are Angels and ghosts, and life after death, and I know there is, then there is a God; and if there is a God, and I know there is, then we are blessed beyond belief. Our wildest dream has come true, even if all of our finite dreams haven't.

I wish I could say that we have all lived happily ever after since the first phenomenal events started happening, that we got settled into an unwavering spiritual life, our financial problems ceased to exist, peace and happiness abounded, and that serenity and an all-understanding radi-ated from us every day since. I could say it, I could pretend it, but it wouldn't be true.

We all dream of happy endings, and on the surface, occasionally it seems that it happens to other people. There was a time I hoped, and thought per-haps my life would start going that way. I would wake up and I would be composed, dedicated, and unwavering in creating a secure, and happy life. I would take charge, be sure of the course, and never falter. I would be a steadfast harbor for my children, and an instrument of service that would please the compassionate and kind Jesus that I have come to know.

But, that never happened, and honestly, my life is still dealing in spec-ulation of what I should do and say, and sometimes the best way just to get through the day, stumbling around in indecision and self-doubt a great deal of the time.

On this oftentimes unsteady road, I discovered that I'm only sure of one thing, but it's everything! I found out that God truly does love us. That He loves us, not in spite of ourselves, but because of ourselves; who we are before the world comes along and starts changing and influencing us. Who our true self is through His eyes; and only God knows that.

I have been unlovable. I have been frustrated, angry, and hell-bent on destruction; even when I didn't truly want to be, and sometimes when I just didn't think that it mattered any longer. Not once, or twice, no, it was so many times during my life that I felt that God was through with me.

Some of my darkest moments came when (well meaning?) acquain-tances, some little more than strangers, helped me to believe that I was more unworthy of God's love than I already felt, and that unless I got my act together and back on the right tract, then I was on a slippery slope to Divine hatred. (It didn't help). When I'd wake up in the morning I was still me. I came back to God, turned away, came back, and did it again.

I came to dislike who I was, and grievous of whom I couldn't be. I fell over and over. I trudged over high mountains of disbelief and despair. I saw Angels, I witnessed miracles, I was attacked by unseen entities, and still I found myself in doubt, struggling, never being able to really fathom who God was, or if He still loved me while all of this was going on.

Through these struggles, I came to believe that this love transcends how we see ourselves, who we think we are, or have been told who we are. We may see ourselves as losers; the world may see us the same way, and be glad to let us know it, but someday all of the world will understand how this loving God can pick us up and gather us to Him, and this time it must stand silent at what the face of love truly looks like.

Did I become "normal," and have I been living happily ever after, after these revelations? Absolutely not. But, you know what? I saw the light when I was blind, I encountered dreams and paranormal activity while I was stumbling around in life, and I was picked up and loved by the Creator of the Universe.

There was a time when I wished for perfection and absolute direction, total assurance against doubt and indecision, but that never was me, and it still isn't. Perhaps that isn't you either. But I learned that not any of us are ever truly alone, we are never abandoned, and we are never hopeless.

It took all of these amazing, strange, wonderful, and sometimes bizarre and frightening experiences to teach me this. There is more to life than meets the eye alright, and believing that we have been personally invited by God to play an important role in an infinite universe is only the tip of the iceberg.

When my granddaughter asked me why I called my book, "Para *ab* normal in Kentucky," I smiled at her, and answered, "Because none of the things that have happened to us are **normal,** and I guess that's just who we are." And maybe it's who you are too.

CHAPTER 1

Wolfe Pen

———— ∞ ————

I ALMOST HESITATE TO COMMIT this narrative to paper. Turning back to the events, and subsequently the terror that my daughter and I experienced had been enough to put it deeply to rest. I did not want it to be part of my life ever again, or my reality. I was so afraid that just thinking of it might once again create the hell that we encountered, and more than that, I didn't want that house to even know that I was thinking about it. Forty-one years later, I still get a dark feeling of discomfort and a not-taken-too-lightly attitude when I talk about it.

My husband, children, and I moved into an old farmhouse, around 1975, which sat deep in the country. My husband had taken the job as caretaker for the wealthy family that owned the property that this house, and their own, sat on. They lived a mile or so through wooded fields. A few other houses were scattered in the area, but at a hidden distance themselves. For those households, it may have been a charming, rustic setting, but for us, we were not so lucky.

When we first moved into the house it seemed ordinary enough. The farmland was spacious, and it was the beginning of a beautiful Kentucky fall. Nothing out of the ordinary seemed possible, and it was the farthest thing from my mind.

I hoped this move might be a good renewal point in my marriage, and that the trials we were having would end. It was not to be. The good times were far too hard to come by, and the bad times seemed to perpetually invade our home life. It was to be the worst year of conflict that we endured, and my depression and anger was at a peak.

The house had two bedrooms upstairs that were across from each other, separated by a hallway that was about five feet wide. The staircase was at the end of this short hall, and led down to the foyer of the front door. The bedrooms were large, so that my young children could sleep in one, and my husband and I slept in the other. We had one twin bed for my son, and two cribs for my daughters.

Since our pullout bed was now in the television room, we needed to buy a bed for ourselves, and slept on a mattress on our bedroom floor until we were able to do so. We slept close to the doorway, which put us about eight feet from the staircase around the corner.

We had only been in the house about one week when there was a strange incident. The children were already asleep in the other room. My husband and I lay down for the night, and soon he was asleep. Being the night owl that I always am, I was wide-awake thinking about one thing or another. I heard a few noises from down stairs that I hadn't noticed before, but figured that it would just take some getting used to the different sounds of the old house.

In the time that it took to think this thought through, I heard a sort of shuffling sound at the bottom of the stairs. It really caught my attention and I stiffened as I discerned what sounded like footsteps. I could hardly believe my ears. Burglary was pretty rare in that part of the country, and I just didn't want to believe that someone would really enter our home. But what started out as "sounding like footsteps," turned into a slow and heavy lifting up and putting down of heavy shoes. Someone was climbing the stairs without any attempt to hide their loud and deliberate footsteps.

For seconds I seemed to be frozen in disbelief, but when the realization really took hold, it jarred me into a spring action. I shook my husband awake and cried, "Someone is coming up the stairs!" My husband, who has never pretended to be the bravest person in the world, but acting out of the shock of being jolted out of a deep sleep, jumped up and raced around the doorway and down the stairs to meet the intruder head on.

I heard him as he reached the landing in the foyer, and then I listened as he searched the downstairs. When he came back, he said, "I didn't find anybody. All the doors are locked, and everything's fine. You must have just heard the house creaking or something."

I couldn't believe that a house could make such odd sounds. In fact, I didn't, but I didn't tell myself that. I let the whole matter drop as though it had never happened. I had enough to deal with in my life without freaky noises invading as well. It was nothing, and that's how it was going to be. That's how it was going to stay. But "something" wasn't going to let it.

Soon, we bought an antique iron frame bed and springs from the classified, a few weeks later. I don't know if it helped aggravate the situation at Wolfe Pen, but it certainly became one focal point.

Times were hard living there. The caretaker's pay was low, and our car was old and unreliable. The disharmony between me and my husband caused sadness and loneliness. I felt in total despair and hopelessness so often that we would never be happy again, and that my marriage was beyond repair. There was a lot of anger in me over this, and a lot of anger at the world coming from my husband. I know now that we provided a great deal of negative emotional fuel for whatever was in that house.

A couple of months had passed, and I was aware that sometimes my son would bounce his rubber ball when we were all in bed, right before going to sleep. Something a little odd struck me about it, but it was just one of those tiny feelings you get, and then it gets lost in the shuffle of thoughts.

One night, from his bed, my seven year old son said, "Mommy, when I throw the ball it comes back to me." He sounded cheerful, but a little puzzled. I walked into his bedroom and asked, "What do you mean?" "When I throw the ball, it stops, and then it comes back to me," he answered. It seemed as though he was looking for me to say that it was "okay."

I wasn't sure what was going on, but I didn't want to make too big a deal out of this, so I just smiled and said that was funny. I had never known Chris to lie, or even stretch the truth. He always played contentedly with his sisters, or whatever toy he had, and this kind of statement really was way out of the blue as far as I was concerned. It was a little thing, but in the pit of my stomach I felt uneasy.

One night, a few months later, we were all in bed asleep. I awoke at the sound of soft crying coming from the children's bedroom. It was my daughter, Jessica, age three. I turned on the light, and comforted her as she stood in her crib. She immediately cheered up, and I fixed her bottle. I stood there as she drank it, and we laughed and made silly chitchat.

A few minutes later I heard a loud noise from the doorway side of the room. It sounded like a loud rushing, or sliding noise, as though something heavy had been thrown down and quickly pulled across the floor, or wall, beside my son's bed. I immediately looked in that direction but couldn't see anything, but when I turned back to my daughter, I saw that her face was twisted in fear. As I stared at her, she pointed her finger in the direction of the mysterious sound, and cried, "Look!" The expression on her face appeared that she was seeing something too terrible for her to see. Chills went through me, and I was on the verge of panic.

Suddenly, ice cold water started hitting me in big drops. It was hitting so hard that it was splashing off of me and onto the floor. I was doubly frightened because it felt so deliberate. It lasted only a few seconds but it felt like an eternity. It took a moment to compose myself, and then I looked for a rational truth. It hadn't been raining, but I knew that water could collect in parts of a roof, and then run down.

I searched the ceiling with my eyes for wet spots, but it appeared to be completely dry. The windows were closed and my two other children lay sleeping a few yards away from me. I went into my bedroom and woke up my husband. "Water started hitting me from out of nowhere," I exclaimed. He was still half asleep, and mumbled something like, "Maybe the roof is leaking." I watched him fall back to sleep.

I felt a little more composed and decided to go back and get Jessica settled. I looked down at the puddles of water around my feet and tried to make some sense of what had happened. Jessica was still standing in her crib looking bewildered.

What happened next made me feel as though I were in the middle of a horror movie. Again, ice cold water started bombarding me. I was being hit from all sides now, and I was aware that I was the only object in the room being so. A fear like I've never known overcame me, for I didn't know what invisible hand was targeting me, or God forbid, if it would show itself. I've never felt so vulnerable, or hopeless against what felt like a diabolical attack.

I raced into our bedroom where my husband was soundly sleeping, and physically started pulling on him. He was wide awake now. "Water is being thrown at me from somewhere!" I cried. As I extended my arms to show him how wet I was, a large bead of water materialized from out of nowhere and splashed onto my wrist. He jumped up from the bed and examined me, and then he went into the other bedroom to examine it, with me following.

I told him about the noise that we had heard, and that Jessica had pointed to something in that direction. "She must have seen whatever it was that made the noise," I said. I was crying in shock and fear. I didn't know if it was going to attack me again, or in what way, or why; and I could only imagine what! By now, the whole house had a feeling of evil that never left until the day we moved. I felt as though my sweet little daughter and I had been the object of some hideous folly, by an unseen foul creature.

The rest of the night my husband and I prayed. I was immobilized by fear and dread. We knew that we really had nowhere to go, and both sets of parents would have thought we were over reacting. My husband's job was part of this package deal, and it tied us to the house in a complicated way, but, from that night on we lived precariously until the day when we could afford to move.

As we took turns praying and reading the bible that night, I felt something hit and push on my side of the bed many times. I was in a state of shock, it was all so scary, and I read the bible, and continued to pray, hoping that God would send it away. I wasn't "safe" in my bed, and just the thought of getting up and walking around that house, putting myself out as a lone target again was terrifying and unthinkable. I didn't know what to do.

We stayed awake all night. My husband got ready for work, and I checked on the children again. After he left, I felt drained and overwrought, and decided to try and get some sleep before the children woke up. But something thumped against the side of my bed several times, and I started praying again. At one point the entire foot of the mattress shook forcefully, and tears started running down my face. I had never in my life been so afraid that I was literally crying with fright. "Why is this happening?" I cried to God.

I moved all of us downstairs. I moved the children's beds into the living room, and my husband and I slept on the pullout couch in the adjoining dining room, that we had made into a television room. Thinking about those upstairs bedrooms during the day was bad enough, but at night it was unbearable.

Jessica started waking at all hours of the night, screaming and crying, as she called for me. While everyone else slept, I awoke and comforted her in that isolated atmosphere. At this point, I felt that she was being deliberately awakened just to frighten both of us. I was as angry, as I was afraid, at the ugly spirit that would reveal itself and frighten a defenseless baby.

Her disposition changed so often to that of unrest and agitation that I didn't know what to do. I interacted with all of my children the same, but my son and youngest daughter showed no personality changes or signs of anxiety.

In the middle of yet, another terrifying night, I sat on the end of the pullout, holding and comforting Jessica, who had just woke up once again screaming and frantic. The television was off, but she turned toward it with a strange look on her face. "Look at the man!" she cried, her little face twisted in fright. I didn't see anything on the screen, but I know that she did.

The entire time that we lived in that house I had episodes of my mattress shaking, and strong vibrations like something rubbing and pushing along the side of it. I prayed and cried constantly in fear of what might happen next. The house had taken on an air of strangeness that darkened even the landscape, and with it, an unknown and unnerving phrase intruded into my mind, one that I had to constantly and willfully fight to shut out, two words that would not leave me alone until the day we left. "Terribia Demonia."

I cringed at the thought of talking about all of this, but in desperation I finally called a priest from one of the local churches and asked him to come over. We told him about the incidents, trying to sound as sane as possible. I didn't expect him to perform some kind of exorcism on the house, or maybe I did, but I just had to tell someone who would understand, someone who would know about this kind of thing.

I told him it was adding too much stress on top of our marital problems. (I finally saw a glimpse of interest.) He didn't seem to believe in ghosts or evil spirits, though, but he felt that if we worked on our relationship all of our problems would go away. God bless and have a nice life! My marriage and my life had gone from troubled to ridiculous, and evidently there wasn't a thing that I could do about it!

We did contact a Pentecostal prayer group, however, a few weeks later, and they actually believed us. Six men, along with my husband, went up to that bedroom and held prayer and bible readings. They said that they felt something in that room, also. I was just so thankful that they believed us.

There weren't any more physical manifestations the remaining time that we lived there. However, I never went back upstairs again except to get a few belongings on the day that we moved, and I never slept on that bed again while we lived there. The house never felt clean or right, and to this day I won't let my thoughts venture back into that house except to answer questions from my family from time to time, and now, in this book.

Life was so much better for Jessica and me when we moved, and I finally felt safe and grounded in a more normal reality. I guess that's why, a year, and a second move later, I felt totally defeated with the reemergence of an invisible intruder. I don't know if it was a new, unfamiliar spirit, or the same malevolent entity from Wolfe Pen that had attacked me and Jessica, but this time, in God's time, a Protector stepped in.

When we moved from Wolfe Pen, we rented a tiny apartment that was close to downtown Louisville. Although my husband's new job had him on the eleven p.m. to seven in the morning shift, the apartment felt the way it should; it felt normal, and I was able to put those horrible memories and fears away, so deeply, it was as though they had never happened. Things like that don't really happen, and they certainly don't happen to us. We were free.

A year later we were able to move into a cute, suburban house in an established neighborhood. One evening, after getting the children into bed, I stretched out also. A loud noise reverberated from the living room. With a small, scared voice, my son called out, "Mommy, something hit the wall." I got up and looked at my children in their beds across the little hallway, and then walked into the living room.

I can't tell you how, but I knew that no one was breaking into our house, and I knew that nothing had accidentally fallen; something had been thrown with what felt like a vengeful force. I could tell by his voice that my son had sensed this also.

I saw my silver cased Zippo lighter lying on the floor, close to the wall. "It's okay," I called out to reassure him, pretending to be nonchalant, "my lighter just fell." I suddenly felt a mixture of anger and uneasiness. Once again I felt vulnerable standing in my own home, I felt singled out. "Please don't let it start again," I prayed.

I wasn't a coward. I wasn't flighty or suggestible. Three years earlier, when we had lived in Indiana, I had walked the country road to our landlord's house, in the middle of a pitch black, bitterly cold night, because our furnace had gone out. At that time, we didn't have a phone, or a car, and my husband was willing to wait it out, but I was worried about my young children getting cold.

The only town was several miles away, and its few stores had been closed for hours. There were only a couple of houses for miles around, and one was way down the road before our house, and our landlord's was the next. It was 1973, rural Indiana, and only woods, hollows, and farmland stretched for miles. It was kind of spooky, but it didn't bother me enough to stop me.

Another time, the children and I had stayed there alone, for two months, while my husband worked around the clock in Louisville, staying at his mother's, in order to save up for our move back to the city. I didn't have a phone, still, or a car, but I was never afraid; or even thought to be. Even at Wolfe Pen, before the physical hauntings started, several times, I had to go out in the dark, country night without a flashlight, into the primitive and dismal stone cellar, to bleed the line of the outdated oil furnace; and only a lone hanging bulb to push back some of the blackness.

Whatever unseen force was attacking and attaching itself to us was beyond my comprehension and strength, and it knew it. I wasn't weak, silly-headed, or cowardly, but I was reduced to tears and weak-kneed terror in its grip.

Weeks passed, and as we went on with our daily routines, I started hearing a familiar sound; the unmistakable squeaking of the antique metal bed springs, when someone sits on them. I would look into the bedroom, and no one would be there. And then, early one morning, while my husband was at work, the end of the mattress shook forcefully as I lay resting. I was too stunned to cry. I had worked so hard to push all of the insanity of Wolfe Pen out of our reality. I had willed that disturbing chapter of our lives closed.

"This can't be happening. It just can't be!" But my eyes were now stinging as I looked around the room; the room that had once felt so ordinary and safe, and I was terrified of what might come next. I truly felt hopeless. "Why won't it leave us alone?" I prayed, feeling my apprehension grow, because it seemed that my prayers had gone unanswered at Wolfe Pen. I felt defenseless against the loathsome entity that was following us.

With my son out of school for the summer, and my husband's late work hours, the alarm clock was now in the kitchen. As I lay awake one night, suddenly a very bad feeling came over me. I had a sense of something dreadful in the room. I wasn't alone.

Just then I heard a sound coming from the kitchen. It was the alarm on the clock. What should have been a reasonable thing seemed intensely frightening. All of those dark nights and desolate feelings of terror flooded over me. I made myself get up and walk into the kitchen. The alarm button was pulled out, although, the time for it to go off was wrong.

"Just a malfunction," I reassured myself, but I was terrified that I would see the invisible thing that I could sense standing close to me in the semi-darkness. In a trembling show of defiance, I took the clock in the bedroom, turned off the alarm button, and plugged it in.

As I lay in bed, I let a few minutes go by, and then I raised my head to look at the clock. Just as I did, the alarm went off, and I jumped up and threw it in my closet. I was prepared to leave the house with my children if it went off again. It didn't, but as lay in bed, I felt mocked, defeated, and stared at.

"I can't do this again," I cried to God, "I can't."

CHAPTER 2

The Aftermath of Wolfe Pen

I HAVE BEEN BACK TO Wolfe Pen since we moved, but only years afterwards, and only because my children and family wanted to see the infamous house. I went most recently, because one day soon the old house will be torn down, and those country acres will be filled with gated community homes. But, I suspect, that won't be all. I pity the person who builds there.

Out of curiosity, a few relatives have taken pictures of the old house, and for the sake of my book, I have gone twice now to take pictures. The day that I went with my ex-husband and his mother, she insisted on taking my picture close to the house. I got out of the car, but I refused to get any closer than way out in the front yard. I managed to stay there for a moment, but that was it. I wasn't comfortable doing that, but never-the-less, she got her picture.

The last time I went alone, was about three years ago. As I sat in the driveway, taking pictures through the windshield, a car pulled up beside me, and a lady rolled down her window and asked if I needed something. I explained that I had once lived there with my family, and just wanted to get some pictures, before the house was torn down.

I knew the old driveway had been reconfigured, and instead of ending at the house, like it used to, it now went all the way to the old main estate of the property, where newly built, wealthy homes have already started to show up here and there.

The lady was very nice and receptive, and stated that she now lived in the estate home. Trying not to give out any facial clues or indications, I asked her if she knew anything about the old caretaker's house. Quickly and adamantly, she replied, "I know that it's haunted, and so is my house. I've heard footsteps coming up and down my stairs."

"Yes," I excitedly replied, "We had footsteps on our stairs, too. Loud, heavy footsteps. They seemed to be very deliberate, and it was terrifying. I thought that someone had broken into our house, and was coming after my family." (It turned out that there *was* someone, or something(s) in our house alright, coming after my family, but they weren't of this world).

Cindy, went on to say that perhaps the hauntings were coming from the fact that the old cemetery on the property had been neglected. It was virtually sunken down, and covered over in the tangled underbrush of weeds and bushes. She thought that the people buried there might be angry because no one had cared about their final resting places. They had been ignored for years.

I felt slightly sick. "What cemetery?" I asked. "The one in the backyard of this old farmhouse where you lived." She pointed in the direction of the back of the house. "You see, back by the fence line."

"Oh, my gosh," I said. I thought of the nights when I had been down in the cellar fixing the furnace pipes, and out in that pitch black yard. Those horrible things that happened in the house, and all of the fear, and worry, and eeriness that had surrounded us. And I never knew that only a few feet away, lay a decimated grave yard.

That fence row was so grown up with bushes and twisted vines that neither I, nor my husband had known that those graves were under there. That might have explained a lot, but not enough. It might not have had anything to do with anything, and yet, that seemed to send a chill through me.

Cindy did not know anything more about the graves, or if they had existed before or after the house was built. She told me that I was welcome to get out of my car, and go and have a look for myself, but I wanted no part of that. It had taken me years just to be able to talk about those hauntings, for fear that it would start all over again. Wild horses couldn't have dragged me out to that forsaken backyard.

It turns out, with a little internet investigating, that the entire land surrounding Wolfe Pen has a very dark and ugly history. One filled with murders, and raids, and massacres.

A few months had passed, when my mother and I were having lunch at a local restaurant. Since she had an interest in the old house, we started talking about the family who had once owned the main estate, a very well-known Kentucky family, and my meeting with Cindy.

We were in the middle of our conversation, when a young man approached us. "I didn't mean to listen in on your conversation, or to be rude, but are you talking about the B_____ family home, and the old caretaker's house that sits on that property?" "Yes," I answered.

"Well, you're not going to believe this," he said, with a rather excited look on his face. "But I used to live there with my family. My father was the caretaker of that property, in the eighties, when my brothers and I were young." I told him that we had lived there in the early seventies.

He was as amazed as I was, and we both said that we had goose bumps, and just couldn't believe in such a coincidence as this. What are the odds? He sat at our table, and started talking about the house. "It's definitely haunted, and you ought to talk to my mother because she could tell you more about it than I can.

He went on to tell me that he and his brothers had the bedroom upstairs, (the one where I was assaulted with the water,) and his parents slept downstairs in the front room. His parents did not talk too much about the out-of-ordinary things that happened while they were living there, but there were things, and they all remembered the night a radio flew across the boy's bedroom.

He wanted me to call his mother, and he gave me her number. The day that I did call, his mother was out, and I talked with his father. He said that he didn't put much time into thinking about hauntings or ghosts, but he did tell me about the radio being thrown across his son's bedroom, and that the house did feel odd to him sometimes. Also, he and his wife both thought that it was strange that the table that sat at the end of their bed would often be moved to a different place in the room. It happened many times.

He told me that another peculiar thing had stuck in his mind, and gave him something to wonder about through the years. When they had moved in, and set up their household items, they had placed two old kitchen chairs at both sides of the head of the bed, just to get them out of the way.

Sometime after moving into the house, it seems that an older relative came to visit, and when she walked into the bedroom and saw the chairs, she exclaimed, "Oh, I see that you are trying to ward off spirits." She explained that placing chairs at the head of the bed was an old tradition that has been practiced for many ages.

Since they had never mentioned the strangeness about the house, that had a bit of an effect on them. They hadn't put the chairs there except out of necessity, but they felt like the result was a little more than just an idea that had come to them, alone. Maybe it came from somewhere else.

They say that time heals all wounds, but sometimes I don't know what to think about that. Less pain, walking around in a numbed state of pain, perhaps not-so-often, pain. Fewer nightmares, maybe.

The experience that I had at Wolfe Pen didn't just scare me, it didn't just ruin a naïve sense of security of this world, it did much more damage than anyone would imagine, and I have never quite been the same, or the same old me, since.

It wasn't physical pain, but psychological pain in the sense that it cut into the very core of me, and it left what I would define as a wariness. It left its mark, more so than any other thing of the paranormal sense that I have experienced.

But in its aftermath, something else happened that I am sure was never meant to occur, or come about from those unnatural and bizarre experiences and spirits, at Wolfe Pen. For whatever destruction was intended, and however painful the fear and the trauma, I can now tell everyone the ultimate story, in my own words, and I have included the most important and significant cast of characters that you can ever hope to meet.

They are all here throughout my book, and I am convinced that they are here to shine a light for your footsteps as well, if you ever find yourself in the dark.

I have included photographs of the house at Wolfe Pen. The first is one of a series that I took from my car. It is of the house, with a few smudges of a light rain on my windshield. Of all the pictures that have been taken of the empty house, this one seems to have captured what appears to me as a ghostly image, looking out of the upstairs window. Although the droplets of rain have added some blurs on my windshield, they are foremost, but the image is definitely behind the wooden frame of the window. The second one in the series, taken just a moment later, had nothing at all in the window, and you can see from the photo, how empty and deserted the house is. Of course, I did not know anything about the image until I had the photos enlarged. I also cropped, and enlarged the photo, so that you can get a better look.

CHAPTER 3

Chloe and the radio

———— ∞∞ ————

AS A CAREGIVER IN THE home of elderly clients, I have had several experiences that were unexplainable in the ordinary sense. I have no trouble, however, when using the realm of the paranormal; for that is what I believe they fall under. One such case involved a 92-year old client.

May lived in a house that she and her husband had occupied for sixty years. They didn't have any children, and her husband had been deceased for years. She was very pleasant, and told me many stories about her life. Because of an old injury to her spine, her shoulders were painfully rounded; causing her to walk doubled over, but she was always kind, in spite of it.

When I first came to work for her, she could sometimes come to the kitchen table with much physical support from me, and her walker. As time went on, she was limited to her bed, with only painstaking trips to the bathroom. These were few, and thankfully so for her, because they caused her much discomfort, trial, and dizziness. After that, she was bedridden.

She was the middle of three sisters, and at the age of 94, the only one still alive. From photographs throughout the house I could see how lovely all three had been. Theirs had been a privileged childhood. Three beautiful daughters, full of life and charm, doted on by loving and happy parents.

Although, each sister had married, only the eldest had had a child, a son that now lived in another state. His mother had passed away early on in his life. The youngest sister, Chloe, came to live with my client after both husbands had died. They built on a great room to hold all of the combined antique furnishings of both households, and stored the rest in the basement.

May told me that with each passing year, Chloe had become more melancholic, and this sadness developed into a severe depression. She would no longer look at herself in a mirror, and couldn't bear that her once beautiful face and healthy body were gone. She saw herself as grotesque and ugly, and nothing could persuade her otherwise. She finally took to her bed with the belief that her life was not worth living. She passed away a few years before I came to work there.

Sometimes when May was sleeping I would study the old photographs and antique portraits. The beautiful pieces of furniture and ornate glass and silver pieces made me feel a happiness of what they once had experienced growing up, and a sadness also for what slips away or dies.

On certain Fridays, I would come to work at three in the afternoon, and stay until Sunday evening. I slept in the front bedroom on these occasions. This particular time was after May was confined to her bed. That night I decided to take the radio to bed with me and tuned it to an old rock and roll station. I put it close to my head and turned the volume on low. May slept peacefully throughout the night.

On Saturday morning I awoke early at the sound of her coughing softly. I reached to turn the radio off, only to find that it had been turned off already. It puzzled me for a moment because I knew that I had not done it. It was an old radio with only a dial in which to tune the station, and one to turn the radio on and off, and it took quite a solid and noticeable click to do so.

I didn't dwell on it, and busied myself with the usual concerns of the day. When I went to bed that night, I turned the radio on again and fell asleep. I got up during the night to check on May and realized that the radio had been turned off again. This time I had to admit what I had already known, that someone other than May, or myself, had turned that radio off; and I was praying that Chloe had a sweet spirit.

I knew that May was in no condition to get out of her bed alone, or push her walker across the wooden floors of her bedroom, the hallway, and my bedroom; and come up to the head of my bed and lean close enough to click the radio off; (and all without me hearing a thing, when her slightest fidgeting during the night would wake me.) She hadn't the strength to do any of the ordinary things that she wanted to do, and her breathing was loud and labored with the slightest exertions.

Out of curiosity, a few weeks later, I asked May if she cared if I used the radio in my room at night. She didn't remember that she still had a radio, and no, she didn't mind at all. I of course never told her about the incidents.

Months passed by. I was sewing curtains late one night and watching television when a loud noise from the basement startled me. There was only one outside door in the basement, but because of the room that was added on above it, it only opened to a concrete foundation wall. From the loudness of the noise, I was convinced that someone had broken a window and was making their way through the maze of antique storage and up to the first floor. I was terrified. I quickly called the police and was relieved when several units showed up and began searching everywhere, careful not to disturb May, who was asleep.

They couldn't find anyone, or any signs of a break-in, however, while I was talking to an officer, I heard the same noise again. "That's the noise I heard," I said, "and I've never heard that noise all of the time that I've worked here." When the other officer came upstairs I asked him what he had done to make that loud noise. "I opened that outside basement door, and had to shut it hard to get it closed," he answered. (I had often felt that Chloe was still around, and now I was sure of it.)

One day, I casually asked May if Chloe had been able to stay at home when she got sick, and she replied that she had. She had died in her bedroom, in her bed, where I slept.

Another day I remarked to May how I loved the many beautiful antique clocks that were all around the house. "Oh yes," she answered, "all of the chimes are so beautiful, especially the big white one in Chloe's room, but I had to quit winding them because Chloe said the music made her sad." I thought about the radio, and I understood.

I was very sad when I had to leave this case for another, and would gladly have stayed with this client anytime, day or night. A burglar, I feared, but never Chloe, and I truly believed that she was still there with us. I believe that she was waiting until her beloved sister could cross over with her. I loved them both.

CHAPTER 4

Dark Spirits

—⟨∞⟩—

IN 1993, STILL WORKING AS a caregiver, I took on what turned out to be a very disturbing case. The client was an eighty-three year old woman who was nothing like my client that I spoke of in "Chloe and the radio." With the blinds and drapes always closed, as she wanted, her house was as dark as her moods, even on the brightest of days. It was partly due to the trees and hillside that it backed into, and partly because darkness just seemed to permeate from the walls and ceiling themselves.

This wasn't my usual thinking or inclination, for I have stayed with clients in bigger, older, and more remote homes, that had rooms like mazes, and yet I was totally relaxed. This house wasn't more than fifty years old, but it had the eerie feeling that time, and yes, even reason, could cease to exist in that depressing residence.

Being a caregiver for many years had conditioned me to disregard harmless rumblings and creaking noises in the night; and not letting your imagination run wild was a must, in order to be comfortable, in this type of night work. In this case, however, whatever force fueled the disharmony and coldness in that house targeted the owner at least once that I know of, and me, in a way that made it impossible to ignore, and even harder to accept.

Miss Jones, for she had never married, had the house built for herself and her sister, who also never married. It was equally divided with a living room, bathroom, and bedroom for each. They had shared the large kitchen, which now had a day bed set up for the caregivers, and where I spent most of my time. A screened in porch backed up to a small, hilly backyard, too thick with ivy and bushes to walk in. This, at least, should have felt charming, and always left me puzzled as to why it didn't.

My client had been confined to her bed for years and was no longer able to stand, but her mind was sound. She passed her days watching only certain television programs, taking a little food, and sleeping. Occasionally she would ask if I wanted to watch a show in her bedroom. This was never pleasant for I had to make just the right amount and content of conversation; for she was disagreeable and prejudiced against anyone who wasn't white, or Catholic; or conversation that was too light, or threatened to be enjoyable.

Miss Jones bragged about the virtues of her mother, which in my mind amounted to narrow minded bigotries and cold heartedness. The sister evidently followed the same. Her father was a hateful man, (she used the word disciplined), and whose entourage of hatred included animals as well. The sisters had moved their parents into this house, in their latter years.

I now must go back to a few months prior to accepting this case. One night I had a nightmare that was so disturbing that it woke me up with a start. I was in a strange house, standing at the bottom of a staircase. A woman standing near me began to say, "Oh how lovely she is. Look at how beautiful she is. She is coming to be with us." I looked up into the dim staircase to see who was coming down the stairs and I saw a woman in an old fashioned wedding gown, complete with a thick veil covering her head and face. It took on a frightening twist when I realized that an old brass birdcage was over the veil. Suddenly a terrible fear overtook me as I realized that the dress was yellowed and ragged. Revulsion came over me and I thought to myself, "She's dead." I wanted to run before they could force me to see what was underneath that awful veil, and to escape that evil wedding party. Luckily for me, I awoke before I suffered too long in terror.

I have always had very vivid dreams with myriad scenarios, so I put it out of my mind. The first time that I walked into the living room of the sister and saw an old, brass birdcage on the coffee table, I felt very uncomfortable. In fact, the entire room made me so uncomfortable that I dreaded being in there just long enough to get the mail from the front door. But I did not yet connect this to my dream.

I worked from three until eleven on Thursday, and double shifts on the week-ends. That meant that I came in at three on Saturday afternoons, and didn't leave until eleven o'clock on Sunday nights. There were no relatives, no friends, and when the light work was done there was nothing to do but quietly peek in on the client regularly, and listen for the baby monitor that stayed on continuously in her bedroom. I kept the speaker with me in the kitchen, where I stayed most of the time, or took it on the back porch where I would occasionally sit.

It was very late one Saturday night as I was watching the little television that I had brought from home, when an odd feeling came over me. Just then, loud snarling and shuffling sounds started coming from the monitor sitting a few feet away. Suddenly, afraid to move, I sat frozen through an eruption of spooky sounds of a child laughing and talking gibberish. The airwaves were filled with the squawking and chattering from a bird, amidst whirling sounds and squeals from what sounded like what I can only imagine, a pig in a slaughter house. Snarls and growls accompanied by some horrible melody from an organ swirled around my already bewildered head. It was all so incomprehensible, and there was nothing to rationalize what I was hearing.

Some people may not understand this, I wanted to turn the monitor off, but I felt as if the moment I tried, something worse was going to happen. Silent tears of fright ran down my face. When I just could not listen, or restrain myself anymore, I jumped up and turned it off.

I needed to check on my client, for after all it was her room where the other part of the monitor sat, and from where all of those noises seemed to be coming. Part of me said that nothing was wrong, everything was normal, and alright, but I was really terrified of what I might find in that bedroom.

I finally gathered the will to walk down the hall and peer into that room. Everything looked in order, but it didn't feel that way. It certainly didn't feel "normal and alright," and I was still shaking. Those horrible noises sounded and felt as if they came from Hell itself.

I did what I've never done in all of my years as a caregiver; I called the night office and told them that I wanted to go home. The night clerk knew this was not like me, and told me to call her again if I heard any more noises, and she would call the police. They didn't have anyone to replace me. After talking to her I felt a little better. Maybe the noises were just static and interference. I didn't really believe it, but I told myself that, anyway.

In a while, I was ready to tackle this fear head on. I turned the monitor back on, with one eye on the television, and the other on the lookout for God knew what. It only took a moment for the silence to be interrupted by the same terrifying and hideous noises. The child sounded devilish with its utterances and laughter. Some type of dog or animal was growling and lashing out, and there were pig sounds of snorting and squealing. That bird was still spewing out unintelligible words and squawks, and the organ music was frightening. This time a cold grip of fear shot me out of my seat and I turned the monitor off. With tears running down my face, I called the police. I couldn't be alone in that house any longer!

The policeman listened to my story, and then searched the house, (except Miss Jones room,) to be sure that there weren't any intruders, and that we were alone. As we stood in the kitchen, he tried to be comforting as I told him how scared I was. At first, he too suggested that it was probably just interference. However, after standing in that kitchen for a while, he looked uncomfortable, and seemed to feel almost as apprehensive as I did. His eyes scrutinized the room as we stood there, and with all sincerity he said, "I don't know what to tell you, but maybe you've got ghosts."

From then on, the first thing I did when I arrived at this client's house was to put that monitor in a drawer. As the weeks went on, on an errand for my client, I discovered an organ in the dark, heavily draped bedroom of the sister. I felt a shudder of apprehension when I realized that the door leading to the basement, located in the kitchen, was exactly like the one in my nightmare, the room and door that had led upstairs. I also learned that my client had owned a parakeet that knew twenty-three words, and that her father, who was a retired farmer, hated that bird.

Neither sister were ever married, and when I found an old fashioned babies' bonnet and stocking in a kitchen drawer one day, for some reason, it didn't feel endearing and sweet, it just felt spooky. You could say that these feelings concerning these items weren't based on reality, but neither were those noises. It was as though everything connected to this house was being used in a hellish, distorted way, in my dreams, and over the monitor.

I continued to work for this client for several months. Partly because I was committed to my company, which was having a hard time staffing Miss Jones, and partly because I determined not to let fear control my life, although the monitor was still put away as soon as I arrived for my shifts.

One spring day, I decided to take it with me, out on the screened porch. It was time to put all of this behind me. I had only sat for a moment, when what sounded like a heavy, creaking door opening, and then slamming, came out of the speaker. I bolted straight in my chair as I heard my client's distraught voice, (she knew nothing about the incidents), demanding, "Who are you? Are you a ghost?"

Suddenly that same menagerie of noises filled the airwaves. I seriously considered running to my car and never looking back, but I couldn't leave my client alone; and not with whatever had frightened someone ordinarily so cold and unmoved. Where I got the strength to walk back into that house and toward her bedroom, I'll never know. The hallway felt as though it were alive, and the atmosphere was so ominous and dark that I don't know how I managed on such shaky legs.

When I entered her dim bedroom, I could easily sense that she was terrified. Even so, when I asked if she had called to me, (to make it appear that nothing had happened,) she remained quarrelsome to me, as usual, and said. "No, I didn't call you." I asked her if everything was alright. She looked around the room as if debating on what to say, or not to say, and then sharply answered that nothing was wrong. I could tell by her entire being that she wasn't being truthful, but I had to let it go at that.

My remaining time on this case was almost unbearable. The fear of being emotionally or physically attacked by some evil force, for that is truly what I believe it was, left me drained and angry. It had happened before; it could happen again. I put that monitor away for good, and there weren't any more occurrences; but there didn't have to be, the atmosphere was set.

It was a relief when my work offered me a full time case with a client who needed special care. To this day I will not use a baby monitor. The chance of something like that happening again is probably remote, and for some people it will never happen, but I know something that they don't, and I'm not going to push my luck.

Conclusion

Through the years, after I had left this case, I would still think about the caregiver that I relieved every other Thursday, and her odd behavior on one particular day. She was never friendly, she never said hello or good-bye, and I don't think I ever knew her name, to be honest.

All I knew was that one afternoon as I drove up the steep driveway, ready to relieve this caregiver, she was standing on the front porch, instead of inside the house, her purse gripped against her with both hands, and some kind of undeterminable look on her face. "Well," I said to myself, "What is she so mad about? Am I late?" I looked at my clock and saw that I was actually a little early. In the time that it took for me to think this thought and to put my car in gear, she was already in her car, backing down the driveway like she was going to a fire.

I always wondered what she was so mad about that day. Agitated and angry enough to wait outside on the edge of the porch, ready to leave at the first sign of her relief.

And then one day it dawned on me. She wasn't mad....she was SCARED.

CHAPTER 5

Child's Play

———— ∞∞∞ ————

AT ONE TIME, AMONG OTHER part time jobs, I earned money cleaning houses in order for them to be sold. This account is about a house that belonged to someone that I knew. I also knew the elderly couple that had owned it previously. It was a beautiful older home nestled in a part of Louisville called St. Matthews. It had charm and vintage beauty, but there was always something a little unsettling about it. My children had remarked that it felt spooky, and I had to admit that it did to me also.

The upstairs had a finished room that must have been a bedroom at one time, but had been a storage area for as long as I had known the occupants. The rest was attic space. Something about being up there was always a little unnerving. You just didn't feel alone.

Around the mid-eighties when it went on the market to be sold, I was hired to clean it. On that day I brought in my cleaning supplies and began working. The day went well enough, although occasionally I would get the strangest sensation that I was being watched. It was an uncomfortable feeling and I did my best to dismiss it and go about my business. I guess that sometimes certain things just don't like to be ignored.

I had filled and emptied the kitchen sink several times while cleaning, but when I tried to pull the rubber stopper out once again, to my surprise, it was so airtight that I couldn't budge it. I tried with all of my strength, and then got a butter knife to pry an edge loose. It was impossible. I was getting very annoyed because not even the softer, outer edge could be pried with several tools.

(I know that all the while I was consciously rejecting the thought that I felt pitted against "something"; I honestly felt that I was, but I wasn't going to let that thought win.) I didn't have any problems earlier and I wasn't going to have any now. But the shadow still came over me that this stopper episode wasn't rational.

When I started getting that eerie sensation that someone was watching me again, I let the stopper be. I turned my attention to cleaning the stove, deciding to let the pressure in the drain subside, for surely that was what it needed to release it. (Hoping that was what it needed.)

The dining room had a swinging door with spring hinges that held it open against the kitchen wall when not needed. It could be closed, and then pushed open with your body if you had your hands full when serving meals. There wasn't any type of locking devise on it.

Suddenly the dining room door swung closed, and it did it with such force that it startled me. There was no logical reason for it to do that. Its spring hinges were made to keep it in place against the wall when it was open, after that, however, you could easily push it with your hand or body. There was at least one-eighth of an inch between the door and door jam, with nothing to hold it; and yet when I walked over and tried to open it, it wouldn't budge. With all of my strength, I couldn't pull it back into the kitchen, or push it open into the dining room.

It was broad daylight on a summer's day, but I felt trapped. I had a strong feeling that once again I was being targeted by some unseen entity, although this time, it felt more like being "played with." But don't get me wrong, it was still frightening. I had no intention of being shut up in a house with something that I couldn't see.

At once I turned toward the back door, when an almost (suggested thought) came to me. "What if that door won't open either?" Rather than fall into that trap, and risk loss of total control of the situation, which is what I felt that I was on the verge of, I backed up and I turned my attention to some other cleaning duty, with one eye checking around the room, and my lips in prayer.

In a little while I mustered the courage and reached for the stopper. It slipped out easily. I walked to the door and pushed on it. It opened as easily as it was supposed to. I don't know which was spookier, struggling against the force that had held them, or having to acknowledge that they had been released.

I've never had to go back to that house, but I've often wondered about it. As uncomfortable as I had felt in that house, and as scared that I was on that particular day, I couldn't help but feel a sadness surrounding it. If I had to guess, I would say a child might be centered, but I truly don't know.

I wouldn't live there, but I don't have any ill feelings toward it like in the case of some other houses. However, one thing I do know is that my idea of a child might not be someone or something else's idea of a child; and I don't have any desire or intention to be the one that finds out.

CHAPTER 6

Guardian Angel

———∝∞∞———

THE LATE SEVENTIES WAS A very troubling time for my husband and me. During this time we started attending a little Pentecostal church that my husband had found. We were Catholic, but sometimes we liked visiting other churches and listening to other people's views as well. I hoped that the structure of going to services together and being with friends of faith might help.

The situation in our home did not get better, and I sent up many prayers and tears to God, and relied on Him for consolation and support through those sad, dark days. The children, aged eight, four, and three, were thankfully unaware of a lot of our problems, and although at times we seemed like a normal, happy family, I feared the reality that it was a hopeless situation.

One night, during a rare respite from problems, my husband and I, a good friend of ours, and our children, were standing around the kitchen table. We were on our way to church that evening, and I was going to sing one of my songs.

We were ready to go so I picked up my youngest child, Heather, holding her in my right arm, close to me. I put my purse strap on my left shoulder, and carried my guitar by the neck in my left hand. I walked out onto the concrete porch in my calf length skirt and high heels. As I stepped down onto the first of the three concrete steps, (the porch was very high, and the steps were big), I became off balanced.

Immediately I realized that I couldn't straighten myself and that I was going to fall. In those frightening seconds I tried to think how I could protect my three year old daughter as we were falling backwards, heading for sharp concrete edges, and a hard asphalt driveway.

Just then, a big, strong hand caught my right shoulder and pressed so firmly that it stopped me from going back any further. It stayed there until I regained my balance and then pushed me until I was standing straight again, with my feet firmly planted.

I couldn't believe it! It was such a close call! And how in the world did they catch me like that, in just the nick of time, and so easily with one hand? I went down the rest of the steps and turned, I just couldn't wait to ask, "Whew, how did you do that?" But just that quickly, no one was there. My mouth was still open in astonishment. "Well, how did they get back in the house so fast?" I said aloud to my daughter. I was shocked by their noiseless speed.

I lay everything down but my daughter, and went back inside where the four of them were still standing around talking. I was giggling in relief at the whirl-wind catch. "Who came outside just now?" I asked. "Nobody," answered my husband. There weren't any special signs of interest. "Who just went outside and came back in?" I asked again. By now they realized that I was very adamant. "Why?" my husband asked. "Because I was falling down the steps and somebody caught me," I answered. "Didn't one of you catch me?" They assured me that nobody had moved since I had gone outside.

We all left for church together and I didn't say any more about it that night. I didn't know what to say. Through the years I have talked about it with my children, and a few friends, but mostly I've kept it to myself.

There was one rare occasion, however, when I shared the story with a co-worker. I noticed that she had an Angel on her bag, and I remarked that I loved Angels. She said that she did too.

Something compelled me to tell her the amazing account of that invisible hand that had saved me and my daughter from a terrible fall. Tears came to her eyes. "You don't know this, but all day long I have been feeling so alone and depressed about my life. When I got on the elevator just now, I actually prayed that my Guardian Angel could give me a sign that he was there with me," she confided. "I thought that maybe he had left me, but I feel like he just answered my prayer through you."

What unseen force had stepped in and saved my daughter and me on that memorable night? Could it have actually been my Guardian Angel? Could I have actually been touched and protected by an Angel of God? It almost makes my head light to consider it, and yet I know I didn't imagine the seriousness of that night. There aren't many possible explanations. In fact, to me there is only one.

CHAPTER 7

To wish for

———— ∞ ————

THE SAME YEAR THAT AN unseen hand had kept me from falling with my daughter, something else happened that was just as surprising, and even more amazing. It involved a most endearing and radiant being that I could ever have imagined, but the thought never entered my head to do so, or that it could happen to me.

I relied on God for comfort and companionship to get through the trying times that my home and marriage were going through, and His loving grace was far more than sufficient, but I found out that we don't know what is in the mind of God or what is around the corner. They always say to be careful what you wish for, and I'm ecstatic to say that in my case it was for prayer.

Early one night in 1977, I put the children to bed and lay down next to my husband, who was already asleep. I wasn't tired, but decided that I should lie there and try to go to sleep. I had closed my eyes for a minute or so but then reopened them.

I couldn't believe what I was seeing! As quiet and peaceful as a scene out of a children's Bible story, an Angel was floating in mid-air, between my bedroom and the children's. I stared in disbelief. Were my eyes playing tricks on me? I rubbed my eyes and refocused. It was still there! I sat up in bed and actually pinched my arm, like they do in the movies, to make sure that I was awake, although I knew that I was. The thought crossed my mind to wake my husband so that he could witness it with me, but I was afraid that if I did it might break that beautiful spell. At this point, I didn't want it to ever end.

It resembled that of a young child, maybe seven or eight years old, with short, curly, blonde hair. It reminded me of paintings that I had seen of Jesus when he was young. It had white, feathery wings that were held back, like a butterfly when it sits on a flower, and there was a glowing halo illuminating its hair. It floated about six feet off of the ground, serenely, with its eyes closed and its hands together, as if in prayer.

There was nothing fearsome or scary about this vision. From the moment that I opened my eyes and beheld it I was enraptured by its beauty and benevolence. It was all sweetness, all kindness. I never wanted it to leave.

I was well acquainted with stories of Angels, and I had a personal idea of how they might look and dress, but instead of the unadorned, earthly white robe that I'd always imagined was standard dress, its gown seemed to glow white; as though electrified with whiteness. On its waist was a wide, brilliant blue band that flowed off to the side. A bright pink sash went up and over its shoulder, and flowed behind it. The colors were unbelievably vibrant on this beautiful Angel of God. Its entire aura, its every detail was more than I could ever have imagined.

I sat, not moving a muscle, silently taking in every aspect of its beauty, cherishing every minute of grace that I was allowed to have. I was so swept up in its splendor that I couldn't even begin to think why it would grace me with a visit. And then, as mysteriously, yet amazingly natural, as its appearance, it was gone.

Through the years I have only told a handful of people. I suppose it is because I felt so unworthy of that Heavenly Being, but also I didn't want anyone to scoff at my story. To me that would have been as if they were calling this wonderful visitor a liar, itself, and I wouldn't have that!

Beside the actual miraculous encounter, the other really incredulous part of this is that after a while I put it deeply away in my heart. I know that it doesn't sound possible, but I did. It became like something that happened in a dream, so long ago.

It wasn't until thirteen years later that the memory fully came back to me, and I remembered it, almost as though I were experiencing it for the first time. It was during a tragedy involving my son that shook me to my very being, when it all came back to me. It's as though it had been waiting, tucked away just for this moment of devastation. Although I don't really know why this happened, or that I was so blessed, this experience has brought me countless hours of joy and awe, and comforted me through many a dark night of sorrow, then, and many years later. Sorrow, I believe, that reached the Heavens.

CHAPTER 8

An Angel with restrictions

———— ∞∞∞ ————

WHEN I WAS GROWING UP cars didn't have seatbelts. And when I was old enough to drive, I thought that they were dangerous. No matter what the statistics said, I wasn't going to be trapped inside a mangled car by a seatbelt. That's what I believed, and nothing could dissuade me. When I had children, I did put them in car seats, although the ones back then didn't really offer much protection. Concerning them, I did what I was supposed to, however, I would remain 'unfettered' in case of disaster because I was convinced that I was right. I remained adamant throughout the years, until thirty-three years later when a miracle altered my thinking.

This miracle occurred in 1981, during the year that I attended Medical Assistant classes five evenings a week.

I had always enjoyed driving. It was relaxing, and I always felt contented whether I was in heavy traffic or on the road alone. But, after I was well into my classes, a worrisome feeling started to hound me. It was a subtle feeling of apprehension every once in a while, but quickly grew to a strong feeling of urgency whenever I got into my car. When I was driving to school it seemed to be at its strongest.

No longer could I drive in peace and enjoy the view. "Look at how fast those cars are going," the thought would intrude. "Think what an impact it would be if they hit you," it would insist.

It was getting to be annoying. "Why am I thinking this?" I wondered to myself, and then I would concentrate on something else. But always another urgent feeling would come, and I would sense, "Those cars are going so fast," or, "Getting in a wreck is so horrible."

I started checking my speed to make sure that I was going a safe speed and being as diligent as I could. This, however, did not make those messages stop. In fact, the more I ignored them; or otherwise, would do to satisfy them, the stronger and more often they came.

This hounding went on, week after week, after week. The subtle feelings went from uncomfortable to distressing. I could not get any relief from this sense of urgency which grew with each car trip. The mental pictures of car crashes, and all of the sounds, motions, and results of impact were ever present. Collision and tragedy seemed to loom on the horizon, and I no longer tried to push the thought out of my mind.

Out of being constantly confronted, my frame of thinking changed. I had tried to dismiss it as natural worrisome thoughts that might come to anyone, but being in a car had never concerned me that way before. No more questioning this urgency, I felt a conviction that I was going to be in a car wreck.

I started praying and asking God to protect me. I would drive as safely as I could. I did everything in my power to ensure that I was out of the woods, but it didn't satisfy the feelings. What more could I do?

And suddenly, I knew. Something that I had never wanted to do, something that was against everything that I believed; "Wear your seatbelt!" It had taken a lot, but for the first time in my life I put on my seatbelt.

When my ex-husband picked me up in his compact car to take me downtown, on this certain week-day morning, I looked over at the seatbelt in his car and saw that it was tangled and twisted beside my shoulder.

On that day, with him in such a talkative mood, it almost seemed too much trouble to unwind it and listen to him at the same time. But I did.

On our way to visit a car lot, I noticed that we were only a block from where I attended college. We were sitting last in line at a red light, when a woman coming up from behind, decided not to slow down, but to switch lanes and turn right. Unfortunately, there wasn't a turning lane, and her brakes suddenly failed as she attempted to stop. We were hit first from behind, and then driven into the car in front of us. The force was so severe, that all three cars in front of us were damaged.

The first impact threw me backwards with enough force to break my seat and slam my head into a heavy tape case on the backseat. With the second impact of us being driven into the car in front, I was thrown forward toward the dashboard. Though it only took seconds, it somehow seemed to be happening in slow motion, for I was all too aware of being hurled forward. Right before the imminent hitting of the dashboard, and possibly out of the windshield, I threw my hands out in a useless attempt to protect myself.

Just then, something grabbed my chest with unbelievable force! It had stopped me when my head was within inches from slamming into the dash. I was stunned, on the point of blacking out, but I'll never forget touching that band across my chest. "My seatbelt!" I thought. I had forgotten all about it, and I couldn't believe that I had it on!

In a traumatized daze I got out of the car and lay down on the sidewalk. I had three large ridges on the back of my head from splitting open the thick plastic case, and whiplash that took quite a few months to heal, but I did heal, and I survived!

I don't know for certain what alerted, and then hounded me until I was forced to wear my seatbelt. I know that it came from some loving and protective being, a force that invaded my thoughts with such urgency and determination that I could not ignore it.

Was it my Guardian Angel, or some other good and loving spirit? Just the thought still amazes me. I had been rescued before when an unseen force had intervened, and I still don't understand why it happened to me, but I live in anticipation of embracing and thanking this invisible companion, one day.

Before enlightenment I chopped
wood and carried water;
After enlightenment I chopped
wood and carried water.

Zen Budhist Saying

CHAPTER 9

Unheard

———⊶⊷———

I DEBATED ON INCLUDING THIS incident which occurred around 1965, under my oddities collection, but with some consideration, I decided that this was scarier than odd, and perhaps needed a little more scrutinizing. I'll be the first to say that it is hard to believe, but whether anyone believes it or not, it actually happened, and I am really at a loss as to why.

It was terrifying at the time, although it hardly seems scary now, at all, and perhaps not very interesting to anyone, except to the person that it happened to; and that was me.

My brother and sister-in-law bought a new mobile home when they first got married. It was comfortable, but back then the walls were a lot thinner than they are now. My mother and sister-in-law were sitting in the living room one Saturday afternoon, as I took a few steps down the hall, and went into the first bedroom on the right. All that separated me from the living room were two thin sheets of paneling, with a few inches in-between.

My mother was sitting on the end of the couch that looked down the hall. It was about four feet from there, to that bedroom doorway, and I was about two feet inside the room. My sister-in-law was in a chair that sat just about where I was, on the other side of the wall.

I had on a pair of Capri slacks that afternoon that had no give to the material, for when I crouched down all the way, to pick up something from the floor, the tightness of the material caused my knee to be pulled sideways, sort of temporarily dislocating my kneecap. I was in excruciating pain, and the strained way in which I was crouching had me immobilized. When I tried to stand, waves of pain would stop me. If I kept most of my body weight on my left leg it would ease just enough to bear it, but I didn't know how long that would last.

I could hear the two of them still lightly chitchatting in the living room. "Mom," I called, "Could you come here?" There was no reply. "Mom," I called louder, "Can you come here and help me?" There still was no reply. I was annoyed, and perspiring in pain. They had to have heard me, I thought, and yet I knew they surely had not. "MOM, SANDY," I yelled, 'CAN YOU COME HERE?" By then I wasn't worried about sounding frantic, I was, and yet when I listened, I could easily hear them still talking about all the little things that people do when visiting.

I just couldn't figure this out. This was just too strange. Neither my mother, nor my sister-in-law would ever have ignored anyone that was calling for help. I was astonished. I was confused. I considered that it was just like a nightmare where you think you're saying something but you're really just mouthing the words. I gave it another round of "HELP, MOM, SANDY, PLEASE COME HERE," as loud as I could. Nothing! I hit on the wall and called again. Nothing! They were still nonchalantly conversing.

My knee was still twisted, and I was at my wit's end. Somehow I forced myself, putting all of my weight on my left leg, to get up. When there was no longer a tight twist on my knee, the pain stopped. I was relieved, however, I felt very strange. Something had happened that made me feel as though I had entered the Twilight Zone, and I couldn't understand it.

I felt scared and vulnerable. I didn't think that I was crazy, but I had just been involved in a really crazy incident, and I didn't like it. I would rather it have been my imagination; I would have welcomed that over the truth. It was as if I had slipped into some kind of 'other' dimension, and maybe I would slip into it again, and it would get worse. Maybe I would disappear like the little girl in that Twilight Zone episode that I had seen years earlier.

It had scared me so badly that I didn't talk about it anymore, or disclose just what had really happened, for years. The few times that I have talked about it, I admit that people usually look at me like I must have dreamt the whole thing. They really don't know what to say or think, and I guess I wouldn't either.

When I gathered my senses, I walked into the living room and asked my mother, "Didn't you hear me calling you?" I must have looked a little unsettled because she looked at me with concern on her face. "No," she answered, "I didn't hear you." "I yelled for you to come help me because I twisted my knee. I called both of you, but you never answered."

They were sympathetic about my knee, and couldn't figure out why they hadn't heard me. (Believe me, they had no idea!) Both of them assured me that they hadn't heard anything. I knew they were puzzled, but I let it go at that.

I'm not sure that they could have fully realized what had taken place on that sunny, Indiana day, or if they could have believed me. I don't know if anyone could believe that sort of thing and be grounded in the real world; at least, not back then, and only if it happened to you personally.

It certainly wasn't any fun, and it didn't feel campfire spooky, or cool in a childish sort of thought. It meant that any old weird thing might happen, at any old weird time, and I didn't want it to. As I said before, it made me feel so vulnerable, like I was somehow temporarily separated from everyone else, and maybe forever. I didn't like that thought one bit.

It was years before I told anyone the whole truth. I had pushed it so far out of my mind in hope to separate myself from it that in time I truly no longer remembered. In fact, it wasn't until I started listening to a radio show called Coast to Coast, in the late nineties, after my daughter and I caught one of its broadcasts coming back from Florida.

Its founder, Art Bell, interviews a variety of lay and professional people who talk on a veritable cornucopia of subjects. The majority deals with the paranormal, and the fascinating range of subjects that it entails. The audience is encouraged to relate true accounts, or ask questions.

A few years ago I was waiting to listen in when I suddenly remembered the incident in Indiana. It had been so long since I had thought of it that as the memory unfolded I had time to consider it rationally. But the facts remained true, even then, and even now. "Well," I thought, "that's something no one will ever bring up. Even Art Bell wouldn't believe it."

Art came on the air and announced that tonight's topic would be on Human Invisibility. I had no idea what that could mean and it sounded a little far-fetched. However, as I listened, I heard accounts of people being ignored for a time as if they were not present, as if no one could see them, and some accounts told of not being heard. There was not one cover-all explanation for what causes these odd occurrences, but I listened to a lot of calls from people who sounded very sane and normal, talking about, and relating fantastic stories of such occurrences in their lives.

At least now I wasn't alone. But, if you could only imagine my shock! I not only found others whom I could identify with, but on the very night that I had remembered it. out of the blue, after all of those years, right before the radio show began.

CHAPTER 10

Angel of Heaven

———— ∞ ————

In 1994, I was working in the home of two elderly clients from eleven p.m. to seven a.m., Monday through Friday. They went to bed early, and when they were asleep sometimes I would stand on their front porch to relax and enjoy the night sky.

On this fall night I was extremely sad. My son was in a very serious situation, and I sorely missed my deceased father. I needed comfort and assurance that my son would survive all that faced him, and that I would be able to find the faith and strength to be there for him, my family, and myself.

As I stood there on the porch, tears ran down my face. My heart was deeply hurt for my son and for the others who had been hurt through this unbelievable ordeal. The pain and fear welled up to an almost unbearable surge and I felt like I just could not go on any longer.

I thought of the Angel that I had seen in my bedroom in 1977, and also of the invisible hand that had kept me from falling. Now, in my deepest sorrow, that all seemed so long ago and faraway.

You wouldn't think that there could be a pain so deep that it could overshadow Angelic visions and touches, but there is, when it involves the life of your child. "Oh," I whispered through sobs, "I could really use an Angel now." But I didn't really expect one.

The moon was full that night and there were only a couple of tiny white clouds that passed in the blue sky. As I stood there studying the houses across the street, a large white cloud came into view in the night sky. Because it was moving rather quickly it caught my eye. From the left part of the sky another large white cloud also moved into view, moving toward the one on the right. This really intrigued me because it wasn't windy at all, and I couldn't understand how they could be moving from opposite directions, and so quickly coming together, one from the left, and one from the right.

In a sort of tumultuous meeting they combined into one massive cloud. It was the only one in the entire sky. The full moon was above, and to the right of it.

The motion of it had my total attention. As I watched, my mouth must have been open in awe. It seemed to be forming a definite shape, and as the motion slowed down and came to a peaceful calm, I realized that it had taken on a very definite form.....a perfect and symetrical Angel stood in the night sky.

It was huge! And there wasn't any guesswork as to what it was, nothing was left to the imagination.

The cloud stayed perfectly still and composed for what I would guess to be less than a minute or so. As I studied it carefully in wonderment, spellbound at its lovely splendor, the tears on my face started to dry. That feeling of never being alone, never being abandoned, warmly embraced me, and I humbly and reverently thanked God over and over for His kindness and tender love.

Once again the atmosphere was full of movement and the heavenly cloud dispersed as quickly as it came. The sky was once again clear and bright blue with the moonlight. Many times I have heard the expression, "Will wonders ever cease?" and all I can say is, "I hope not!"

CHAPTER 11

The swinging hangers

———— ✀ ————

As I HAVE WRITTEN IN other stories, the winter of 1993 was a time of disturbing dreams and nagging feelings that something was wrong, or that something terrible was going to happen, but I didn't know what. I was beginning to think that it may involve my son, and considered many times to warn him, but when I thought it through I figured that I would just be worrying him over nothing. He seemed happy, worked every day, and shared an apartment with his friends. I didn't know what to say.

This incident occurred around May, of 1993, while I was sitting on my bed reading some papers. The sun was getting ready to go down but I had not turned on the light. There was still a little sunshine coming from the window where I was sitting, but it was dim in the corners of the room.

My three-year old granddaughter had walked down the hall and was a few feet away from me. I started to speak, when a noise coming from the closet caught our attention. Its door had been removed because of some remodeling that I had done, so had the clothing, but lots of hangers remained.

When I looked toward it, I saw that a few of the metal hangers were swinging back and forth, and then simultaneously the entire closet full of hangers started swinging back and forth, wildly and loudly. It was a scene of energized commotion.

Out of the corner of my eye I could see that my granddaughter looked up at me. I looked at her to get an idea if she was aware of what was happening and if she was seeing what I was. She opened her mouth as if to say something, but we both just turned our eyes back to the closet.

The whole incident lasted about twenty seconds or so, and then one by one the hangers individually slowed down, and then simultaneously they all stopped dead. The way they stopped swinging back and forth by themselves was just as mind boggling as how they had started.

My granddaughter and I looked at each other again for a moment, and then I walked over to the closet. I looked to see if perhaps some clothing had fallen off and started the chain reaction, but I knew that couldn't have explained what had happened.

Something did catch my eye though. In the dimly lit left hand corner, against the wall, a jacket was hanging. It was my father's. I had brought it to my house after he died, because he had worn it for years and it still smelled like him. I slept with it when I was sad, and wore it when I felt blue. I must have left it there when I removed the other clothing. I stood for a moment just looking, and then I hugged it.

As odd as this may sound, nothing about the situation was scary. I didn't have the urge to turn away, or to flee the room. I didn't feel like I had to protect Elizabeth, or that she was even frightened; there had to be a loving spirit behind it that made it so. As the hangers clanged noisily, my granddaughter and I had stood spellbound in the midst of something amazing, the way you might feel while witnessing a brilliant cascade of shooting stars.

The only troubling part was that I felt as though my father was trying to tell me something but I just didn't know what. A few days later

I noticed a photograph of my son that was lying on my dresser, and I picked it up. For some reason unknown to me, I started crying. "Oh God, Chris," I whispered; a despair that I had never before experienced flooded over me, and tears streamed down my face. I literally felt as though my knees could buckle beneath me. I sobbed uncontrollably for a minute or so, and then, like waking from a bad dream in the middle of the night, I slowly wiped my face and gained my composure. I felt drained, but like so many bad dreams, it was over with. Or so I thought.

CHAPTER 12

The new tires

———⊰⊱———

DREAMS CAN BE FRIGHTENING WHEN they bring news of trouble and turmoil. They can shake you to your very soul when the shadows of forewarning drift over you in the middle of the night. But there is no doubt that dreams can also be fascinating and amazingly beneficial. Either way, whether they are lighthearted or disturbing, dreams that give us information before the fact are psychologically intriguing. Not only can they pull information seemingly from "thin air", but they can also distribute this same information on more than one person.

The idea of two individuals intimately linked to one another's dream-state- consciousness is fascinating, and I was once again taken aback. I discovered that two people could share the same dream, on the same night, not once, but many times. I have really enjoyed contemplating this remarkable twist even more so since this involved my daughter and me. This was all discovered by "accident", although I am wondering if there is such a thing!

A few years ago I dropped in on Kitty, my ex's mother. She told me that she was just thinking about me, and was about to call. All morning she had felt compelled that her mother, who had died a few years before, wanted her to help me in some way.

Just then she looked out through her picture window at my car. "I think you need some new tires, don't you?" She thought about this for a moment and then cheerfully added, "I think that's what mother wants you to have."

"Oh," I said, "that is SO strange because I dreamed of her last night." In my dream she wanted to give me something. I told her that was really nice, but she didn't have to. She was insistent, "I want to do this for you." Suddenly we were in a busy train terminal with lots of people rushing around. I realized that she was carrying a suitcase, as we hurried to get her aboard a train. Her husband who had passed away several years before was going with her.

Kitty exclaimed, "My goodness, you don't realize HOW strange that is because Heather just called and left a message on my answering machine. She had almost the exact same dream." She then played the message from my daughter. In her dream, (this was the first time that she had ever dreamed of her great-grandmother,) the two of them were at a busy airport terminal. Her great-grandmother was leaving on a trip. (I've often wondered if the difference in traveling accommodations was because my daughter enjoys flying, while I've always fantasized traveling by the old passenger trains.) Her grandfather was there also, just as in my dream.

There is a third part to this account which ties it together in an amazing way. Kitty had no way of knowing that only a few days before I was longing for a new set of tires. I had been looking at the new tires on a car parked next to me and thinking how threadbare mine were, and that I was afraid they were no longer safe. I knew that it would be quite a while before I could even think of buying any. I didn't pray for tires, as I recalled, but I was addressing my conversation to God that day. I was hoping that the people beside me could be doubly blessed to appreciate how fortunate they were.

Later, Heather and I discussed the strange coincidence of having had similar dreams about her great-grandmother. A few weeks later we found ourselves sharing another dream.

While visiting one day, she said, "Oh, I had a really bizarre dream last night. I was in Paul's house, (my neighbor who had recently died of cancer) and he was still alive, but his face looked like he had been in a horrible accident. I ran over to the phone to call 911, only I couldn't get through. The phone wouldn't work right. Someone else was there with me trying to help, I think it was Chris. I wonder why I dreamed about Paul that way?" she asked, "it was so scary."

I told her that I didn't know why, but maybe it was a representation of the cancer. The oddity of it was that I just had the same dream, with the usual exception that I was the one in the dream. Someone was with me also, it wasn't clear in the dream but I thought that it was Chris, as well, as I had recalled the dream when I awoke that morning.

A few weeks later she asked me if I had ever dreamed of Debbie, a friend of her fathers. "Yes, just recently," I answered. In my dream I went to visit Debbie and found out that she had just passed away. I was looking at her bedroom and saw that she had all kinds of needlepoint and embroidery projects lying around. It really made an impression on me because to our knowledge she never did any type of sewing. Although I didn't know her very well I decided that I should go to her funeral because she didn't have much in the way of family or friends. I stood out in a hallway at the funeral home and talked to a lady about how sad it was.

"I just knew it," exclaimed Heather. "I had the EXACT dream, except once again, I was the one in it. When I woke up, I thought, I'm going to call mom. Something just told me that you had had the same dream." It was a few years later when Debbie did pass away.

One day when my two daughters and I were visiting each other, just sitting around talking, Heather said, "I just remembered a dream I had last week. It was so strange. I was at Nanny's, and suddenly someone was announcing that a volcano was erupting, and I could see lava flowing toward her house. Everyone in the neighborhood was trying to escape by car, or else on foot. I was just trying to decide what to do as I watched the red hot lava flow all around."

Jessica and I listened as she recalled the dream. "Isn't that an odd dream?" Heather asked. Jessica and I looked at each other, and I answered. "Yes, it is, but what's even odder is that I had the very same dream last week and had already told Jessica about it." "You're kidding," Heather replied. I went on to say that the dream was exactly the same, with the peculiar detail that I was the one in my dream, and not Heather. It was such an unusual dream because my mother lives in Kentucky and volcanoes are never given any thought, and because my daughter and I shared it. (I can happily say that nothing has ever come about of that last dream.)

My daughter Jessica, and I shared an event in our dreams, a few years ago, with different aspects as the focus. Before what subsequently happened, for the last month and a half I had dreamed of the ordinary things that one comes up with in the R.E.M. stage of sleep, although with one noticeable difference. In these eight or nine dreams my little dog, Mercy, would be sitting or lying next to me. There wasn't any unusual context to speak of except that I had never dreamed of her before, and now, suddenly there she was. After the third dream of her, I started to worry a little. After the fifth or sixth, I patted her head that morning and said a little prayer. The morning after the ninth dream, as I petted her lovingly, I prayed again that God would send His Angels to protect her.

I wasn't aware that the night of my last dream of Mercy, my daughter had a vivid dream that her neighbor was standing out in the street. Her neighbor was crying because she had been involved in some type of an accident in her van. (Jessica feared that Tara must have had an accident and injured her children, because she was so upset.) The dream ended with my daughter trying to comfort Tara by telling her that it was alright, that it wasn't her fault, and that we knew she couldn't help it.

On this particular evening when my grandchildren were talking to the neighbor's children at the front door, I noticed that Mercy was standing at the door also. As I walked over to make sure that she didn't run out, as she was inclined to do, she made a dash through their legs and flew across the street, just as the neighbor, Tara, drove past. We watched helplessly as the van's back tire hit her, full on, throwing her underneath the van. Another neighbor helped me carry Mercy to my daughter's car. She was terribly injured.

My daughter couldn't reach her own veterinarian and was desperately trying to find the number of an office that would be open. The lady that hit Mercy was crying and saying how sorry she was, as she helped my daughter look through the phone book. "It's alright," my daughter said, trying to comfort her, "It wasn't your fault. Mercy ran out so fast that no one could have stopped in time. It'll be okay." (Jessica later told me about the dream that she had. She could hardly believe how it had all played out, when she thought about it later that night.)

Mercy was very lucky, and surely must have had a little Guardian Angel with her that day. Although the tire had hit her fully on, it somehow flipped and threw her under the van without catching her beneath it. She had life threatening bleeding in her bruised lungs, and had suffered a major blow to her right side, but after three days of oxygen and I.V.'s, and a lot of prayers, she was able to come home without one broken bone. Even though the healing process was slow and painful, and the veterinarian couldn't promise that she would make it through the first night, or week, she made a remarkable recovery.

For many days I had to keep her confined in a big plastic tub when she came home because she was still in danger of bleeding to death in her lungs, and I stayed close by her side day and night. Just like in my dreams, she was lying right beside me every time I looked down. I thanked God for those dreams that gave me a chance to say a couple of heartfelt prayers for her life. It is a miracle to all of us that this little dog is alive and well.

My son and I shared a unique dream experience while he was imprisoned one hundred and fifty miles away. On a visit with him, he told me of a sad and curious dream that he had about me when he took a nap one Wednesday afternoon. In the dream I was in a dimly lit room. The only things that he could recall seeing were a lot of stuffed animals in the corners. I was standing in the center and I looked very sad. I kept saying how tired that I was.

I listened in wonder, and with more understanding than he realized. "Yes," I answered, "I was in the big bedroom where I used to sleep. I have moved out almost everything except for a few things. Elizabeth's toys, and a lot of stuffed animals are piled in the corners. I was working in there that Wednesday, and thinking of you. I missed you so much, and felt so tired and worried. I even spoke your name out loud as I wished you could be home." (This was also the bedroom where my granddaughter and I watched the hangers swing wildly in the closet.) Chris acknowledged this with a pensive and understanding nod.

There have been too many instances in our lives to cite, but two other particular times when this tie of consciousness was apparent will always stand out in my mind. One, when my son was about fifteen. He had stayed at home with the neighbor's children while I was out. He had a serious bicycle wreck, flipping over the handlebars, and landing so hard on his back that he almost lost consciousness. Another time was when he went swimming with those same neighbors and burst his eardrum while diving. Both times I immediately knew that something was wrong. No amount of assurance from my husband could relieve the fear and distress that I felt, and I had to get home immediately.

I don't know how emotional and physical events can transverse distance and consciousness, but I do know beyond any doubt that they can. My children learned early in life that our family had a psychic bond that not everyone realizes, or believes in, although it has become as natural to us as breathing in and out.

CHAPTER 13

In dreams I walked with you

—⠿—

CANDY AND I HAD BEEN close friends since we were young. She was unbelievably funny, smart, and so full of life, that I couldn't wait to see her when we were apart. When we weren't giggling and tormenting each other with our silliness, we would lie on her bed and read poetry, or sit cross-legged out in her driveway at two o'clock in the morning singing, "I'll be looking at the moon, but I'll be seeing you."2

One night she appeared in a dream. She was sitting in the living room of my neighbor's house, and she looked ill. Although there were no words with the vision, I knew that she had died.

That was the entire dream. It seemed so real. I told my daughter about it, and that I needed to spend more time with Candy. With work, and now living a distance away, I had lost a lot of time with her in the past years.

A short time went by. One night when I was visiting my cousin, she remembered that my mother had called earlier, and mentioned something about Candy being sick. I immediately called my friend's number, and her brother answered the phone. "Did you call my mother?" I asked. "Yes, we've been trying to reach you. Candy is dying," he sadly replied. She had been diagnosed with a fast growing cancer only months before, and had just gotten home from the hospital under Hospice.

I got to be with her for the last three days of her life. She and I were alone in her living room as I sat by her bed, and I just couldn't believe that I would have to say good-by to this precious gift that had been a part of my life for as long as I could remember. I was gently rubbing her arm when she took her last breath. I whispered her name, but I knew that she was gone.

Paul had been my neighbor for twenty-three years, and lived next door to the right of me. Our yards and homes were more like one, in that we had bonded so closely. He was a friend and neighbor, a brother and father, all rolled into one. He never locked his door, whether he left for work, or if he went to bed. He wasn't afraid of burglars, but mostly he always wanted to be sure that if I needed anything that I could get in. That's the kind of friend that he was. I would often call him from work, when things were slow, just to hear his gentle voice. He always ended our visits or conversations with, "Okay, hon, I'll be here if you need me."

Seven months before his death, I dreamed that I walked into Paul's house. (The same house that Candy had appeared in, dying only one month before Paul.) It seemed so strange that all of his things were gone. The familiar pieces of furniture, the pictures, that were always sitting in just the right spot, they were all gone! It was as though I was actually there, seeing for the first time how it looked, now that it was empty. I wondered, as I looked around the empty house, why I felt so detached from the reality of it all. For some reason, I was resigned.

Paul told me a few days later that he had been fighting a sinus infection for a few weeks, and his doctor had ran some tests. I couldn't believe my ears when he told me that he had cancer in his throat, and at the base of his brain. Over the next seven months his weight dwindled down, and he lost the fight for his life.

I first met the woman who had bought Paul's house, when she came running over for my help. Paul had told her that I was a bit of a handy-man, and she needed me to turn off the main water valve in the yard. Her icemaker line was leaking and was flooding the kitchen floor. After turning off the water, she invited me inside. She had not yet moved anything into the house. It was as though I had stepped back into that dream! As I looked around at what once had been an inviting, loving home, I pushed my feelings deep down, because I had barely begun to deal with Candy's death, and I didn't dare let my guard down now. I resolved while standing there, to not "feel" anything; to not let this even be Paul's former house. "Yes," I thought later, "that would explain how I felt in the dream." I could fully understand it now.

Anna Mary is my paternal grandmother, and I have never met her, at least not in the ordinary sense. She had died of cancer when my father was a young soldier. My maternal grandmother had told me that I looked just like her, but that was about all that I knew of her, when I was young.

One night, when I was a teenager, I dreamed of her. In the dream, she looked like the picture that daddy had. I was running around, having fun at a small, county fair; there were a lot of farmers and their families enjoying the day, as well. It was so clear. I saw my grandmother, and ran to where she was sitting, in what looked like an old fashioned, wicker wheelchair. She had her left leg resting down in some type of wooden, whirlpool bucket. She smiled lovingly as she wrapped her arms around me, and kissed me. I felt so happy.

The next morning when I walked into the kitchen, I told my mother about the dream; the odd wheelchair, and that something seemed to be wrong with her leg. My mother thought that that was interesting, because my grandmother had suffered a stroke sometime before she died, and it affected her arm and leg. I had never known that, nor did I know that she had used a wheelchair, and it was just like the one in my dream.

It made the dream so valuable to me because I had learned information that I felt came straight from my grandmother. I had never considered that she might know and love me, and I think this was her way of letting me know.

Sheron is one of my dearest cousins, but throughout our married years I didn't see her as often as I did her sister, Sandra. But they are not only my cousins, they are my sisters, and best friends, all tied into one. I loved them dearly because they could be as silly as the three Stooges, or as pensive and poetic as any Wordsworth or Hemingway. We laughed and cried over the same hurts and made-up jokes, with the same heart. We could not only finish each other's sentences, but many times, we knew what the sentences were going to be before we even said them. Growing up, we didn't appreciate that we had a very close psychic bond; to us it was just the way it was. It turns out that it ran in our families.

When I started having dreams that Sheron was ill, I asked Sandra if she thought her sister was seeing a doctor regularly. She said that she believed that she was. I asked her to be sure and tell Sheron to take care of herself. I had several more dreams about Sheron having serious problems in the chest area, and each time I would ask Sandra how her sister's health seemed to her, being that she was a nurse.

After each dream, I would tell Sandra that I was worried about Sheron having serious health issues. We only knew that she had some problems with what appeared to be acid-reflux, based on what her doctor had diagnosed.

The final dream in that series was very vivid. Sheron was seriously ill, and complaining with upper stomach and chest pain. Suddenly, she began to have a heart attack, and I watched powerlessly as she was taken away.

Even though she had been checking in with her doctor, the last dream convinced me that something was seriously wrong with her. My mother called a few days later to ask if I knew that Sheron was in the hospital. I was distraught, but not surprised. Her husband had taken her to the emergency room during the night with what seemed to be severe stomach pain that went into her chest. The diagnosis was critical, and she required by-pass surgery. It had been her heart all along.

It is more than a helpless feeling when you are sure that a loved one is in danger, and there is nothing that you can do to cause that person, or in this case, a doctor, to take serious action. My cousin did survive, however, and I am very thankful for that.

The dream that I had of my Aunt Iva and I, going up the stairs in the old farmhouse, was similar. She told me that she was having pain down her arm. She said that she just didn't feel well, and was having a lot of difficulty with shortness of breath. I found out a short time later that she had undergone complicated heart surgery. Thankfully, she survived also, to be with us for many more years.

After a while my dreams began to include people other than my immediate family, and then extended out to people that I barely knew, or did not know at all.

One dream involved the father of Tony, one of the policemen which my daughter was friends with. I had only met this friend a couple of times, briefly, and had no idea if his parents were well, or if they were still living. I hadn't given it any thought. One night I dreamed of Tony's father. I was in a house that I had never been to, and met someone that I understood to be Tony's dad. The rooms were crowded with people, and for some reason, as hard as I tried, I couldn't seem to make sense out of what was being said. The scene switched, although I cannot tell you to what, but I realized that Tony's father had died.

The next time that I saw my daughter was at a Christmas gathering. We were all talking, when I remembered the dream. "Oh," I said, "a few nights ago I dreamed that Tony's father died." She had become used to the idea that in our family, dreams could very likely hold importance. "Tell me about it," she said. I gave her all of the details that I could remember, and then added that the conversations were very hard to understand, and to make sense of.

She leaned forward in concurrence, "He has Alzheimer's." "Well, that would explain the confusion," I surmised. She said that she would call Tony and tell him about the dream as soon as possible. "I'm not saying that this will definitely happen, but if there's anything that he needs to tell his father, or that he needs to hear from him, in whatever way possible, then perhaps he ought to take care of it now," I suggested. "I know," my daughter agreed, "just to be on the safe side."

It turned out that Tony and his father had never been close, and nothing had changed for the better when his father became ill. Visits had remained strained and infrequent. Tony had mixed feelings as he listened to my daughter's words of warning, but decided to make an extra effort for his father's, and his own sake.

Although he had Alzheimer's, Mr. Smith was seemingly in good health, without any physical problems; nevertheless, he died two months later. Tony later told my daughter that he was glad that he had taken the time, and made the effort to be with his father as much as possible, and that it did help in finding closure. He was grateful for the dream, and my daughter and I were too.

Several years ago, through friends, my daughter Heather became acquainted with a young woman. Although they were to become close friends as the years passed, she really didn't know Claire (as I will call her) very well, when she approached Heather, and told her of a series of reoccurring dreams that she was having about her father. She had come to Heather because she had heard her talk about some of the dreams that I have had of significance warnings, and of being able to offer occasional help in clarification, and so she asked my daughter to relay the dreams to me, and see what I could come up with.

It is not too hard to reason that when we have occasional dreams of our loved ones, we may feel that they are concerned for us, or have something that we wish they could tell us, but when dreams become so persistent and constant, invading our nights and filling our days with worry, then we get a sense of frustration and urgency when we feel in our hearts that something out of the ordinary is happening. Claire was at this point with her dreams.

The dreams were very simple, and consisted only of her father, and were basically always the same. Just as in my dream with my own father, he always appeared to be saying something very important, something that couldn't be heard. And although she tried with each dream to understand what it was that he was saying, and to speak to him, she never could.

Initially, I am never sure if there is more to the obvious, or the human understanding of how we perceive life, but I told her that just off of the top of my head I would say that there is something that she needs to hear from her father, and that there is something that he needs tell her. The dreams were his way of trying to communicate.

I could understand her unease, for in the dreams he was very troubled, very worried, and distraught, and although he was trying desperately to communicate with her, there were no words coming out of his mouth.

She seemed to be able to appreciate the offering, and confided to Heather that her father had committed suicide a few years before, (something that we didn't know) and agreed that she did need to hear from him, and had so many unanswered questions. She had struggled very much because this tragedy was so incomprehensible and painful to her.

She went on to say that with the relentless sadness and agony surrounding his death, there was one particular day when she had been working outside in the yard, that it was all just too much. It was one of those hot days when you feel like there is no air, and her pain was so overwhelming, that she cried out to God that she could just not go on with her life if He didn't take this crippling pain away. She was paralyzed with the sorrow. Just then, from out of nowhere, the wind picked up, and a strong, cool breeze swept over her, and miraculously the pain was gone, and the burden lifted. Completely and continuously. Her prayer had been heard, and answered at that moment.

I was certain that this was the basis of her dreams, and was probably a pretty good conclusion as to what they were about. Yes, you would think so, but as I have so often experienced, we can never guess what may be around the corner, or how the story ends.

As her new acquaintance was just going through a divorce at the time, there were times when Claire's friends would worry because she would show up late for work or other occasions. After one very long absence, those who knew her were really getting worried. She finally opened up and confessed that her soon to be ex-husband was coming to her house, wanting to argue and fight about the divorce, and often preventing her from leaving her home.

One night Heather had a dream that was so vivid, and the details so brutal, that it was startling. It was as though she were on a glass floor, looking down on the other people in her dream, which was Claire and her soon to be ex. In this dream, the man called Claire and told her to meet him in some obscure location, and that he had something of hers.

The dream changed, as Heather watched, and she was looking over a wooded location. She could see Claire's body lying there, as though it had been carelessly discarded. She could see her friend's entangled hair, and her crumpled body, as though it were so real she could touch her. She was dead, she had been murdered.

It is hard to tell someone, especially someone that you don't know all that well that you had a horrible dream about them being murdered, and by someone that they know. It does not always come off as so easy, or smart, or welcomed like on the television shows that would make it appear more acceptable, or normal. Claire had taken in my dream consideration, but this might not go over so well. Heather risked going from helpful, to being that weird person that you might want to avoid. She was in a dilemma.

In the end, although it is hard, it is harder still to keep quiet, and not tell someone; especially with what my family and I have been through, and lessons that we have learned. These types of premonitions, and dreams, and gut feelings of events that feel likely to happen just won't be dismissed, won't let you be, and won't let you get them off of your mind. And thank God they won't.

Heather told the dream, just exactly like it was, leaving nothing out, or trivializing any part of it. She told Claire, emphatically, over and over, "If he calls and asks you to meet him, tell him NO!"

Claire had not heard from Randy in a while, but a few days later after the dream, he called, instead of showing up as usual, uninvited to her house, where she would try to appease his anger. He demanded that she meet him in an out of the way location on the pretext that he had something to give her. With Heather's dream still on her mind, Claire was startled and taken aback, but she didn't hesitate to clearly speak up, "NO, I will not meet you anywhere. If you have anything that belongs to me you can take it to the local Police Station and leave it there." Of course, he never did, and thank God, that was the end of it all.

She later confided something that she had never revealed to anyone, concerning a day in the beginning of her divorce, when Randy had showed up with a shotgun, and laid it on the kitchen table. He had never been physically abusing to her, but on that day he didn't offer any explanation of why he brought that gun to her house. Suspicious, she didn't ask out of fear of what the answer might be.

That was around the time when she started having the reoccurring dreams. I know for certain that not only did Claire's father care deeply about her, but enough to watch over her throughout the years, enough to flood her with dreams, enough to call in two outside persons who would be receptive. If my daughter had not spoken up and taken the risk to warn her friend, it could have been a very different story for all involved. I know that these dreams saved Claire's life, and in doing so, gave her just what she needed to hear from her father after his untimely death, that he loved her, and that he was still with her, and that there is hope in life, after all.

Claire is just an ordinary person, just like me, and my family. And I bet just like you. And I think it is by far one of the most wonderful things in the world to be just an ordinary person who finds out that they are important, and cared for, and thought of by a most extraordinary God.

The night before September 11, 2001, I pulled onto Interstate 75. It was evening as I started on my way home from Berea to Louisville. I had settled myself for the two hour drive, and was thinking of happy memories of the visit. Suddenly a heaviness came over me. A deep sadness flooded my heart, and I began to cry. I had nothing sad on my mind, and I was in a good mood, yet I was so overcome with such emotional pain, that all I could do was sob with all of my being.

It occurred to me that it wasn't the first time in my life that this had happened, the other time being when I picked up my son's picture before his arrest. I began praying for family members as the immensity grew deeper and stronger. Praying wasn't lessening the pain as waves of emotions and the fear of enormous suffering surrounded me.

I wondered if it were possible that World War III was going to start, or if there was going to be some catastrophic disaster, like an earthquake or volcano. Something so horrific, with massive loss of life seemed eminent, and I didn't know in what direction to pray, or for whom. It was overwhelming, and I sobbed on and on. I prayed for humanity. I prayed for our country, and for the blessings that had kept the enemy away from our borders for so many generations. I prayed for everyone and everything that I could think might be impacted by a disaster. I prayed that we wouldn't have that disaster.

A sorrowful verse from the Bible came into my head; "Jeremiah 31:15" came to me. "A voice was heard in Ramah, lamentation and bitter weeping, Rachael weeping for her children, refusing to be comforted, because they are no more." The sadness that I was experiencing was overwhelming.

My tears finally stopped, and the last heavy breath had eased into a regular pattern. I looked at the clock on my dash. I had cried for forty minutes, desperately seeking a release and a solution to this query. My heart was heavy the rest of the way home, and I felt that once again I had been drawn into events that had not yet occurred, and given just enough information to scare me to death. I didn't tell anyone about the ride home, but I was pretty sure that something terrible was about to happen. I couldn't imagine what, or to whom, and I continued to pray.

Only a few nights before, in a dream, I found myself standing in the middle of a large city. I was looking up at the skyline when suddenly one of the tall buildings burst into flames. I was at a total loss at what to think when the building next to it also burst into flames. The dream ended there.

I started to mention it to my family but it just didn't seem relevant, I guess you'd say. It was just one of those odd dreams you have and you never know where they come from. I didn't give it any more thought. It may seem strange but I didn't recall that dream at all for some time. I was getting used to the fact that dreams had played an important role in my small world of events, but I never "dreamed" that they would continue, or expand to include an entire world. This completely amazed me, but what amazed me more was that I never thought of that dream again, not until months after the World Trade Center towers were hit.

When I got in from my distressing trip, I had another dream that night. I was in a familiar, though unknown house. My youngest daughter was in the bedroom, ironing. I walked to where she was, and looked at the news broadcast that was on the television. I couldn't entirely make out what was going on, but there were scenes and descriptions, such as during wars and catastrophes.

In the dream, I started telling my daughter that we should all be very thankful for the freedom that we have, and that we don't realize how easily it could be taken away. I talked about the soldiers and private citizens who have died to protect us, and our freedom, and that we should never take for granted the price they have paid throughout the course of our history.

The next morning, before I had time to turn on the television, my neighbor asked me if I could believe what had happened. I listened in shock as he described the attack on the World Trade Center. He had no sooner told me of the first building being hit, when a second airplane exploded into the other tower. Words can hardly describe what everyone in this country felt at that time, and I walked to my car muttering and moaning in emotional pain.

I had already planned to visit my daughter, so I drove on to her house. She had her television on, and met me at the door asking if I had heard what was happening. As we sat and listened to story after story of devastation and death; heroic flights of firemen and policemen, friends and strangers risking their lives to save as many of the victims, in what could only be described as a scene right out of hell, we cried.

And then it came to me, I was saying all of the things that I had said in my dream. It was all relevant to what was going on, right then and there. And being transfixed on the news, it had become almost impossible to know where the dream had left off, and this morning nightmare began. With this act of terrorism, the flood gates of war, and suffering, and loss have swung wide, and deep, and there are many mothers who are weeping for their children, and cannot be comforted.

Of all that God has shown me I can
speak just the smallest word,
Not more than a honeybee takes on
his foot from an over flowing jar.

Mechtild of Madgeburg

CHAPTER 14

When God talked to me

— ◦◦◦◦ —

WHEN MY FATHER DEVELOPED ALZHEIMER'S, I never questioned why. Illness was not an animal that stalked its prey, with a life of, and unto itself. It couldn't have understood the question, much less answer it. It wasn't an attack, but the inevitable breaking down of a vulnerable and mortal life, with all of its frailties.

Dealing with the heartache of daddy's suffering was painful, it was horrible, but just like death, it was not alien to life, it was a condition and progression of life. Three years later, my sweet and loving father was dead. I was devastated, I was heartbroken, but I never thought to question why.

God was the creator of life, and the keeper of the secrets of our soul, and I couldn't, (and never will) believe that He instigates problems, accidents, illnesses, or our demise. I never felt that He caused my father's illness, or that He had given him an Alzheimer's cross to bear. I didn't believe that He needed him up in Heaven more than we needed him here, or would lay waste to him and everyone who loved him, just to get him there.

It was just life. I believed, and still do, that God is all hope, all good, and all steadfastness, and that He welcomes us home when our mortal bodies give up our spirit. It was just the way life was, sometimes horribly sad, and always fatal.

It was odd, though. As time passed and the pain of losing my dad settled in for the long haul, I began to feel isolated from the everyday world in so many ways, and this isolation made me, in turn, lean on my father's memory and spirit, even more. At first this gave me great respite, but then I began to seriously wonder if my father were truly alive and happy in a new, heavenly dimension, or was it all too good to be true? This doubt spread to the very existence of God. Was He too good to be true as well?

I had started a journey to remember, and hold onto any remnant of my father that I could, but suddenly I wasn't sure which road to take, where it began, or what frame of mind I should I be in to best serve my purpose. I became confused on that road. I became lost. Did I really know the way? Did I ever really know God?

The tighter I tried to grasp the unseen, and understand the unknown, the less I could realize the truths that I once rested upon comfortably. I had lost my father, and suddenly I felt that I had lost God, too.

In my front yard, where my children and I lived, was a pine tree, the baby of the first Nursery Christmas tree that my father had planted, when I was nine years old. He had cultivated and protected it in his yard, simply for the enjoyment of my children and me, and then brought it to us when it was about three feet high.

I could never have guessed, as I watched my father carefully working that day that he had only seven years left on this earth, or that this tall, beautiful tree, that brought such joy and comfort, would also be instrumental in bringing me to a starting place on my way back to faith.

We lived out in the country, at the time, and had neighbors around us, but after midnight quietness covered the rural setting. The stars were unbelievably beautiful because we lived far away from any industrial lightning, and you could see the silhouetted wooded hills for miles around.

Seeking comfort late one summer's night, I sat down in the grass under the soft, fragrant branches of this tree, which now stood 13 or 14 feet, and sorrowfully and hopelessly sought my father, and my God. My head was full of questions, and my heart of sadness. The memory of those wonderful miracles that had happened to me in the past had somehow been deeply buried and forgotten.

Should I run to a Church? But which one? Somehow I was all burnt out. Won't I just find the same old answers that I've heard all along? If I try one more time and I fall short, I'll only end up feeling more guilty and estranged from God. "I just don't have what it takes to be a good Christian. I'm not reliable or consistent," I thought. "And so often, church only makes me feel more worthless and unworthy." I wasn't sure if God really existed, did I need to feel that I was an abomination as well? (Maybe humans did invent gods to believe in just so we could fool ourselves into believing that we're not alone.) "I'm so afraid that you are not real...."

"Shhh...Be still." This thought came to me, but I disregarded it. I didn't need any unconscious, useless suggestions from myself. "God, if you can hear me, I'm scared...."

"Shhh...Be still. Be quiet." (It didn't seem like my own thought, but it must be.) "Why am I thinking this? I'm in turmoil, I'm in distress, and I need answers."

I have always had a hard time understanding where God was in proportion to my small life. If He was in my heart, then He must be a concentrated energy. He also must hate being near me when I sin for I was taught that He couldn't stand to be where sin was. Did He run away every time I was unjustly angry, or when I cursed, or was just generally bad? Even when I felt that I was having a pretty good day, I still couldn't feel Him. Had He forgiven me for the hundredth time, or was He still angry and purposely staying away because He knew that I was going to sin again, sometime in the near future?

Was He as tired of the ordeal of coming and going to avoid my failures, as I was of worrying about it? Now I not only felt lost but I realized that I was angry at God. (That seemed dangerous and preposterous,) but I just couldn't indulge this crazy sort of sadistic-masochistic doctrine anymore. "Wasn't He supposed to be the strong one? Wasn't He able to handle reality? Shouldn't He have understood how humans were before He created us?"

As fallible and weak as we can invariably be, we sometimes have to go through hell and back just to make it through to the end. Was He so fragile that we were constantly breaking His heart, even when we didn't mean to, when we're not even able to protect our own? If we had to face the horrors in the world, then couldn't He face the horrors in us? If God couldn't realize and accept this once and for all, then He wasn't a god at all. With tears running down my face, I felt the last desire to believe in anything, slip away.

"Be still"... (It was not an admonishment. It was a gentleness that one uses on a much loved child who needs comfort.) *"Be still, and I will tell you everything that I want you to know."* This time I couldn't dismiss it. A breeze came across my entire body, which caused the soft, dark green branches of the pine tree to sway all around me.

"I know that voice," I thought. It wasn't an actual voice that I heard out loud, it wasn't a voice coming from some unbalanced part of my mind. I can't explain it, but it was like a strongly whispered, silent thought. It was a voice that could speak the universe into existence, a voice that commanded respect and attention; a voice that sounded like love itself, in motion.

I was in a state of rapture as an all-encompassing wonderment and peace spread over me, and yet I was acutely aware of my surroundings and the unbelievably beautiful night. It was as though each breath I took filled me from head to toe with life, as it strengthened and consoled me. Suddenly I became aware that I was no longer just breathing in this wondrous Spirit, but that we had become one, and this Breath permeated everything that was, or had ever been. I too now touched and breathed with all of creation.

"See how big I am." (Always I had fitted Him into the dimensions of my heart, and when I felt He was absent, I had pictured Him somewhat misty and limited, although I knew that He was supposed to be omnipotent.) I never wanted to admit it, but in lieu of nuclear bombs and unfathomable hatred, it just didn't seem likely that God was big enough to manage this world. I had always hoped that He was, but it just didn't seem likely.

I closed my eyes and tried to picture a God-like figure larger than my house. *"Bigger."* The voice coaxed gently. I pictured the same figure as tall as the sky. (This time my imagination was reinforced with a reality that came from outside of me.) *"Bigger."* The voice felt like a living breath that permeated every part of my body as it spoke.

As this was happening I began to sense a profound reality of God restoring my faith, and healing the pain and doubt in my heart. As my faith grew, seemingly so did God. It was as though God were living and working from inside of me, and then growing larger and larger, keeping me safe inside of Him, as He grew. I had never imagined anything like this, and on my own, I had never dreamed of God in this context. I now could comprehend how complex and powerful God could be; understanding that this was just a minute reflection of Him.

"Bigger," the voice again coaxed. I now felt God enveloping the universe and all that one could possibly imagine it contained, as I was staring into the night sky and breathing in truth with a certainty that I had never thought possible. I was caught up in a wide-eyed, wide-awake ecstasy. The importance, the significance of it all was monumental and breathtaking. It was also humbling; emotions could not express my gratitude. It was

as though each breath that I breathed heightened and strengthened this new awareness. **"Bigger,"** the voice whispered to every muscle, bone, and sinew in my being.

"Everything that is, is in Me. I am a sea that all creation rests in. I am beyond, and bigger than anything that you can imagine. Everything that is, rests in Me. You cannot lose Me, or cause Me to leave you. There is nowhere that you can go that I am not. No matter how far you sink in sadness, despair, or failure, you will just sink deeper into Me, and I will comfort you. You are always in Me, and safe in my love."

In a way that I had never contemplated, had never envisioned, had never hoped, God told me that He was willing and able, big enough to take care of all that He had created. And then, as though touching my face with His, He said that He truly was the ALPHA and the OMEGA. He still was "I AM."

"I am bigger than you could ever imagine, and yet, see how very much I care about you. I know your thoughts, I am present in your every moment, I have seen every teardrop that has fallen, and I understand you. See how very much I love you."

I'm not sure how long I sat and silently pondered all that had happened without putting any of my own words to those thoughts. These were tremendous revelations that had been disclosed to me, and the magnitude of it all was so overwhelming that I could only sit in silence. I was in a state of rapture. I sat outside in the moonlight for several hours that night just taking in all that had happened, and all that I had learned, never wanting to leave that spot of Heaven on earth.

I was not always constant in my beliefs throughout my life. I was not always faithful, and I did not always believe that God existed, but in the still of the night, or in the midst of these spiritual storms, the one prayer that never changed, was, "Please God, just don't let go of me." He never did, He never has!

For the next three nights I sat with God under that tree, and listened to all that He had to tell me. I know that He is waiting for you, in a place of solitude, or in a crowded world of turmoil, and He is able and willing to tell you everything that He wants you to know.

"Be still, and listen!"

CHAPTER 15

Angelic Calling Card: 11-11

———— ∞∞ ————

THERE ARE A LOT OF people talking about the 11-11 experience, nowadays. In the last few years, I've heard countless people, on television and radio talk shows, tell about their personal experiences with these numbers. In fact, a few years ago, I learned that a close friend had the same belief that the numbers 11-11 seemed to be everywhere that she looked, day or night. Unfortunately, her life was cut short, and we never got to talk about it.

Going back a few years, I could not have imagined that ordinary, common numbers would be used as a catalyst for awareness and hope, but early in 1993, I started on an amazing journey that at first had me baffled and at a loss for answers. It took a year or so for me to accept the fact that something deliberate was happening.

At first, I thought little about the odd coincidences of seeing 11-11 everywhere: at cash registers, as room or book page numbers; strangers asking me for the time and it always being "11:11." "That's all it could be," I thought, "odd coincidences." But as the first year ended, the phenomenon didn't, and I was beginning to feel a little perturbed by it. It was past the point of thinking that it was just a coincidence, and the more I went out of my way to pretend that it was my imagination, the numbers "11-11" would literally jump out at me from unforeseen, or near impossible situations.

One particular incident happened as I finished watching television in bed. I turned it off, turned over, and was ready to drift off when something fell off of my night table, although "fell" is not what came to mind, and I knew that from the start. I lay there for a moment and thought about ignoring whatever had happened until morning, but I couldn't. To me, it had sounded as though my car keys had been tossed up in the air before landing beside my bed.

I rolled over and looked over the edge. There was the oblong, brass key ring with my keys, lying on the floor. I had placed them on my table when I came in from work earlier that night. They couldn't have been 'barely' hanging on the edge for hours. They weren't wrapped in a leather band that somehow 'unwound,' and sent them over the table; particularly not jumping with a flying leap. As I looked up, my eyes met the face of my digital clock; 11:11. I somehow knew that I was being summoned into phase two; no more ignoring, no more doubt; someone, or something was calling.

I kept all of this to myself for two years or so, still thinking that it would end without an explanation, and no one need worry that I was turning neurotic. It didn't end. Over a period of time, one by one, I started asking my children, my cousin, and a few others, if the numbers 11-11 meant anything to them. I always asked casually, never too over-inquisitively, and I always got the same answer. Those numbers meant nothing to anyone that I would ask. I felt discouraged at this point, for I was now sure that those numbers meant something, and I just didn't get it.

Finally, one night while the television was on, and I was busy around the house, a show that I occasionally watched came on. It was called "Strange Universe," and it had stories from the Angelic, to the paranormal, to the just plain bizarre. I heard the announcer ask the questions, "What is the strange phenomenon of the numbers, 11-11? And why are they calling people from all over the world?"

I could hardly believe what I was hearing! I raced to the television and waited anxiously for the commercials to end and the show to start. All of these months and months of feeling alone with something that I knew was really happening to me, but couldn't fathom that such a thing was possible, or could actually have a meaning when it seemed so unlikely; now to find out that it was happening to other people, and was going to be talked about! It just baffled my mind. I literally was beside myself with anticipation.

It seems that this phenomenon truly was worldwide, and evidently was growing. Some new-age people on the show felt that it was heralding in an age of new-birth for our world and us. Some felt that it had to do with dimensions opening that would combine the spiritual with the humanistic and physical world.

All of this seemed to encapsulate a lot, but the explanation that clearly spoke to my heart was that the Angels were using the numbers 11-11 to get our attention, in preparation of great changes that were coming, and that a time of spiritual growth and love was needed to prepare ourselves, and our world. They were launching a front, if you will, to let us know that we are not alone, that we are important, and that God is still with us.

When the television show ended, I sat on the floor filled with unbelievable excitement, turning the words of the announcer and each contributor over and over in my mind, as though they were describing a priceless treasure that had just been placed in my lap.

A few days later while I was checking in on a friend's dogs, while he was working, I flipped through the television channels only to catch the end of a story that a young singer was telling to Regis and Kathy Lee, about numbers. "My grandma always taught me that when the numbers "one" line up, the Angels praise God.

I could hardly sit still in my chair. "When the numbers line up, the Angels praise God." I rolled the words over in my mind. Once again, on world-wide television, someone was talking about those numbers! "Angels," I said out loud. "When the ones line up, the Angels praise God." I was beside myself with joy and anticipation. I now knew beyond any doubt, that the circumstances and occurrences of the past two years were not only real, but were for some reason being carried out by heavenly Angels, and I was included in this unfathomable pact. I was both thrilled and bewildered by it all, and I was humbled to my very being. A puzzle in progress was clearly poised in front of me, but now the pieces were coming together.

Today, in 2017, it is not hard to find books, television specials, and memorabilia about Angels, but in 1993 awareness of these wonderful heavenly creatures wasn't so main-stream, or acknowledged. All of the major Christian religions taught us that angels existed in historic religious context, and that they were created by God, but one really had to go to the Catholic Church to find a more personal affection for these special messengers.

Even the people who had had personal experiences with what they believed to be Angelic encounters, myself included, hesitated to talk about them. As I stated in some of my other stories, I stored my experiences in my heart so deeply, not knowing what else to do, that eventually it was as though they had never happened.

When the numbers 11-11 starting jumping out at me, something else started happening as well. Angels! It seemed that everything had something to do, or was about Angels. I had always loved Guardian Angel stories, but no one was talking about them. In those last two years they seemed to be in my thoughts a lot, and I started noticing Angel references in so many of the things that ordinarily I wouldn't. It seemed that everywhere I looked some Angelic suggestion was there. Whether it was a word, or a physical symbol of some type, I began to see them continuously.

At this time I could never have guessed that "Angels" were launching a worldwide campaign and were about to burst on the scene in a big way. The time had come for these beautiful messengers to be heard. Soon a world full of people would be talking not only about Angels, but the numbers 11-11.

I can only tell you what this experience says and means to me. I believe that Angels are as real as you and I, and that they have individual personalities with wills of their own. Early on in creation some evidently chose to follow Satan, an Angelic being with a dark, ungodly side, and they all were banished from the Heavenly realm, and God's love. Those Angels who chose to be loving and loyal companions to God are blessed and powerful spirits, who not only look after their Creator, but those of us on earth, as well.

In as much as they are pure and loving, they seem to have a free hand in watching out for us, and the freedom and ability to step in and offer all kinds of help. Most of us by now have heard or witnessed accounts where seen or unseen forces have intervened just in the nick of time. We have been consoled, guided, and protected by these Heavenly beings, and most of the time we aren't consciously aware of it. Only when the unimaginable happens, when from out of nowhere, someone, or something steps in, and we are miraculously saved, do we truly start to believe that the Angels are all around us, and that they love us.

I believe that the Angels, having the luxury of being able to watch us from both a physical and spiritual spectrum, birth to death, are more understanding and loving than we can imagine, and because of their purely benevolent spirits are more than willing to help us when circumstances allow.

I do believe that from what seems like the most insignificant to the most important, our life choices and patterns are set in motion for our ultimate spiritual growth, and all of heaven must not, by right of our free will, forcibly intrude upon us. However, I see the Angels as a gift from God to help ensure that we continue on these paths for our ultimate good. Rather than ask why the Angels don't protect us from all disaster or heartbreak, we can be thankful, that whether they appear in a miraculous moment, or watch undetected without our knowing, that God and His Angelic guardians are near, and devoted to our well-being.

I believe that great physical and metaphysical changes are coming to our planet. Prophets and scientist alike have been warning us that our world, our universe, is about to undergo drastic weather, geo-physical, and spiritual transformations. More importantly, Jesus warned us about these things two thousand years ago. It's true that we have always had tribulations, this earth is no stranger to disaster, but I am talking about tribulations that have had no precedents, a time when the spiritual meets the physical in a culmination of events and awakenings like none other since the beginning of time.

I believe that we are living in a time that is like no other, and that we now, and as the age progresses, desperately need all the help that we can get.

Angelic calling card: 11-11. What does it say to me?

<u>Time is of the essence. Fear not, for you are not alone. God has not deserted you!</u>

CHAPTER 16

The 444 Experience

—— ✦ ——

ONE NIGHT, IN LATE 1999, I had a series of dreams that seemed so real that I felt I was actually present in them. In one, I found myself sitting around a campfire at night, amidst a rugged landscape. I, and a group of people were talking and laughing heartily with Jesus. We loved Him so much. He was our Rabbi, and we felt loved and safe in His presence, just happy to be near Him. He was so wonderful. Though the night was dark and the landscape barren, it was ecstasy to be sitting there.

(The dream changed), and I was standing at the bottom of a steep hill, at dusk. Someone walked up from behind me, dressed in a long, roughly-woven garment. He reached out His hand to grasp a rock, to help give Him an anchor on the steep hill that He was about to climb. He was so familiar to me that I recognized Him by His hand, (even though He had not yet been crucified.)

(The dream switched once again), to a group of Jesus' followers asleep on the ground. I was lying fairly close to Jesus, who was also asleep, and I was slightly touching the edge of His robe. Because I was Jewish, it suddenly occurred to me that it might not be acceptable for a woman to be camping out with the men. But I didn't stir because it was so comforting to fall asleep knowing that our Rabbi was near, and in touching distance.

I wondered if I should wake Jesus and ask His permission, but I was afraid that I might have to leave, (and I couldn't bear to do so.) I lay very still, and watched Him as He slept. Immediately a large, digital clock readout covered my entire vision. It read 4:44.

The next day the dreams were still very vivid in my mind as I shared them with the client that I worked for. I found myself lost in deep thought every now and then throughout that day, and still do, to this day, pondering the realness and clarity of those dreams. They were so comforting, and somehow they felt more like wonderful memories, than just dreams.

Several months passed, and one evening when I was mindlessly wandering around a store, waiting on my daughter, I found myself in the book section. My eyes settled on the book directly in front of me. It was "The Messengers," by Julia Ingram and G. W. Hardin. I had heard something of this book, and Mr. Nick Bunick, and had supposed that it was probably about Angels, but that was all that I knew. Since that was a favorite subject of mine, I took it home.

I had just begun to get settled into it when the numbers 4:44 jumped out at me from the pages. I recalled my dreams, and excitedly read Mr. Bunick's account of Angelic awakenings at the hour of 4:44. It also chronicled events concerning Jesus, which he believed he had personally witnessed while in a past life. This was simply too amazing and unbelievably exciting. I couldn't put that book down until I had read every word.

Although his experiences were unique, it reaffirmed to me that my dreams of Jesus, combined with the digital readout of 4:44, were somehow more than just dreams. Just like 11-11, 4:44 was to become particularly important to me, and people from all walks of life, scattered all over the world.

God has entrusted His holy Angels with a mission. Beyond a doubt, there is an important message for all who will open their hearts and listen; one that is for the good of mankind, and the glory of God.

CHAPTER 17

An assortment of oddities

———— ∞∞∞ ————

I HAVE FOUR GRANDCHILDREN, ELIZABETH and William, and Zackary and Luke, and not to leave out, a great grandson, Rory. Like so many other people who have experienced this amazing love, I am very close to them. This story happened when my granddaughter Elizabeth was around six years old.

One sunny afternoon, unknown to me, my daughter Jessica was visiting her mother-in-law, with her two children. Phyllis's house is located in a suburb with a big backyard that slopes down to the creek. It connects all of the other yards on that side of the street.

That same day, my cousin and I were out on a drive, when I suddenly had the feeling that something was wrong. I was contemplating what everyone close to me might be doing, when something happened to me that had never happened in quite this way, or this strongly.

Mentally, I could clearly see from the yard sitting catty-corner, and behind Phyllis's house. It was as though I were looking out through another person's eyes, very low to the ground. (In my vision), I slowly walked into the creek and came out into Phyllis' yard. I studied Elizabeth as she looked in my direction, and then listened as she started calling for help. I heard her call several times, and then she disappeared into the house. I continued to walk, and then I went off through another yard, without further incident, and the vision was over.

At this point I somehow knew that all danger had passed, although I was perplexed at what had just happened. I had been praying the entire time for all of my immediate family, and then intuitively for Elizabeth, just to make sure that God's Angels were standing by for assistance.

The next time that I was visiting my daughter and her family, Elizabeth excitedly told me about a scary time that she had recently. "I was out in grandmas' yard, when a big dog came across the creek and walked toward me. I started calling for help, and then I ran into the house." "I know!" I said, "I saw you!" "How did you see me?" she asked. "I don't know, I just saw you in my heart, I guess." She pondered this and then smiled contentedly.

My daughter explained that she had been out in the side yard when she saw the dog. It evidently was just a big, sweet dog, not out to hurt anyone, but my granddaughter, who was in the backyard, didn't know this.

Somehow her feelings of fear had not only trans versed the physical dimensions of her mind, distance as well, to come to me, but had crossed a barrier that took in a third party, one that was not even human. How I came to see through those animal's eyes, (for that seems to be exactly what happened,) I'll never know. It is an incident that has mystified me for years.

This might have really been hard for someone to understand if they had never been exposed to the myriad stories that my children and I had shared throughout the years, but for my grandchildren it was just one more interesting and comforting conformation that they were being watched over in more ways than any of us could begin to comprehend. Personally, I am very thankful.

While writing this book, I have delved deep, and awakened feelings and memories that are ever amazing, and yet, even more amazing is what all I had forgotten; had never pieced together, or seriously took into account in the importance of my life.

One particular incident happened over forty years ago when I was a very young, and unsophisticated seventeen. I had decided to apply for a job at Lakeland, an asylum for the mentally ill, that sat in a semi-rural area, a few miles from my house. It is now renamed, and the turn-of-the century brick buildings have long been replaced with multi-complex modern ones.

Naive about jobs, I was untrained and unfamiliar with this facility and what it required, as I pulled into the parking lot. The receptionist directed me to another building and suggested I wait for the facility bus, but in my excitement, and thinking that it could not be far, I decided to walk. After walking for quite a distance, my hands and feet started to burn in the cold air.

I had not realized that the temperature was in the single digits, and I was dressed only in a cotton dress, slip, and a too light-weight coat. With only hose and slip-on flats, my feet were almost numb by the time I turned to look at the building that I had started from, and was alarmed as I realized how far away it was, but that where I was going was even farther.

Every rush of the stinging, bitterly cold wind went through my inadequate clothing; my hands, face, and feet were almost stiff, and I could not remember ever being so cold. I felt scared as I looked around. I had been walking for a long time, the grounds were deserted, I was out there all alone, and I knew that I had made a big mistake.

Out of the corner of my eye I caught sight of another building. It was a lot closer than the other two. A wave of relief came over me, although I felt I wouldn't even be able to reach it before I froze to death. I walked as fast as I could on stiff feet; pushing myself with steadfast resolve, all I could think with each crunch of the frozen ground was to get inside.

Finally I reached the building. Finally I would be safe and warm. Anxious and without thinking, I grabbed the doorknob, but before I could turn it, a firm voice in my head commanded, "STOP!" "DON'T OPEN THAT DOOR!" It stopped me dead in my tracks, but I didn't have time to think about or analyze this odd thought, I was freezing to death. Again I reached out for the doorknob. "DON'T GO IN THERE!" The voice, with an almost parental quality, was commanding. This time, without under-standing or knowing why, like a programmed child, I obeyed. Wrapping my arms around me, I finally made it back to the building from where I had started. I never did apply for that job.

Many years had passed when this memory came back to me and I shud-dered to think what might have happened if I had hurriedly, innocently opened that door and gone in. What I didn't know on that noteworthy day when I was seventeen, was that Lakeland was seriously understaffed, and the patients were often left alone in large, open wards while the staff attended other duties. I also did not know that the doors in those build-ings were meant to be opened only from the outside, and once you were in, you didn't get out; and only if you could locate someone with a key.

Some of the buildings housed patients who were quiet and unthreat-ening, while many were volatile and potentially dangerous, but the building that I had since learned, that made even the staff leery and kept them on their guard when they had to enter, was the one that housed some of the most dangerous and psychotic patients of all, the criminally insane.

On that day, I hadn't known what building I had chosen. It was one that was smaller, and set apart from the others. I didn't know what I would have found inside, or what would have happened, but *Someone* knew, and swiftly prevented me from entering. And I have whispered many a heart-felt thank-you throughout the years for their protection.

CHAPTER 18

Tall, dark, and Angelic

———— ∞∞∞ ————

IN THE EARLY EIGHTIES, MY children and I were living in Oldham County, Kentucky. During this time, I took a mechanic's class for eight months.

One night, after attending a party given by a student in that class, I started for home. His house was inside the Louisville limits and because I had experienced some electrical problems with my head lights on the way there, two young men offered to follow me until I made it home. I only knew the one, he was also taking the class, and the other, an acquaintance of his, I didn't know at all.

As it turned out, this other fellow was an unscrupulous type, into selling and using drugs, and rumored to be dangerous to the point that eventually my class mate had to distance himself from him. It also turned out that my classmate wasn't all that trustworthy, so that was saying a lot. But I did not know that at the time, and because I was very naïve back then, never considered them to be anything other than friendly guys who were looking out for me.

I had made it out into a small town when my head lights went out, along with all accessory power. Figuring that my alternator must be bad, I parked my car at an empty church, and they offered to drive me the rest of the way home.

As we talked I started feeling uncomfortable with their views and opinions about various things. I was anxiously looking forward to getting home when we realized that one of the back tires had gone flat. At the time, I was new to the area, and we were, for all practical purposes, in the middle of nowhere. It was after two in the morning by then and if anyone lived in the vicinity, there wasn't a house or barn light to be seen to show it.

This was a narrow, infrequently traveled, secondary highway that eventually went past a small town, and then eventually led into another smaller town. That was it. In those days, that road only winded out into miles of small farms and woods. Any fork that you took eventually only led to another small town, closed down at this time of the morning. Without any major highways or interstates to hook up to, the expression, "You can't get there from here," explained it. People who didn't live out this way just didn't bother, and after two in the morning, there was even less reason to be wandering around.

You have to realize that this was before home computers and cable television. Life was very different back then in those small, poor, southern communities. There were no sophisticated societies, no swinging liberal parties that offered a wide range of personalities; and the black citizens still lived off from the white ones, mentally, as much as physically, and the only people who were well off were a few who had good farms, or lucky enough to have a good job worth a commute into Louisville.

Back then, white people who were financially stable ran the communities, and set the standard for day to day living. Poverty ruled the rest of us, black or white. Especially the blacks. And that is why what happened that night was such an unusual situation, and has given me many hours of intriguing contemplation.

As I said before, I had already started feeling uncomfortable in the company that I was in and didn't relish the thought of being stranded with them. As the driver located his jack and spare tire, I stood in front of the car trying to stay out of the way, and only making small talk when they spoke.

Suddenly a car drove up, from out of nowhere it seemed, and pulled in front of us. In the light of the summer's night I saw what looked like a car right out of a show case. It was a beautiful, brilliantly white Cadillac. Its interior was also white, as was its convertible top, which was down.

My eyes could hardly believe it when I saw a pair of fancy longhorns mounted on the hood, from what must have been a gigantic steer.

Out stepped a tall, well built, handsome black man. Not only did the outfit that he was wearing look expensive, but it was like something from a western movie. His fancy shirt, tailored jacket, and slacks were white and went over what appeared to be white boots. His outfit was topped off with a white cowboy hat.

He strolled past the two men and came over to me. "How are you doing tonight?" he asked. He had an air of strength and calmness about him that made him seem unworldly. "I'm fine, thank-you," I answered shyly, at this kind stranger. He stood beside me for a moment, and then said, "I just thought that you could use my help," in a way as if he already had.

And then, like some nauseating scene from a 1940's Selma, Alabama newsreel, the driver, with jack in hand, replied, "Oh, I think us white boys can take care of this." Anger and humiliation washed over me at being entangled with these traveling mates, and I glanced at the man beside me, hoping that he hadn't heard the ugly remark.

He had heard alright, and the look on his face is one that I'll never forget. He was smiling. We all stood motionless for what seemed like an eternity as this stranger stood smiling at the driver. It was a smile that seemed to fear nothing, and understood all. It was as though nothing could diminish the love that emanated from him, as though he were smiling at a child with unrealized possibilities. No one, not even the smart-aleck driver could speak a word.

Fear and outrage are words that we use so many times during our lives to describe events and people, but clearly this man had neither. His countenance could not have been more above us if he had been floating ten feet off of the ground. I know this may sound strange but it was as though we could barely comprehend him.

He turned his attention to me again, as if he'd known me all of my life, and said, "Well, I just thought I'd stop and see how you were doing. You all be careful." I thanked him appreciatively, and then watched as he got into his car that was headed toward the country, and drove off into the night.

I thought about that night many times throughout the years, and then eventually it became a stored memory; that is until eighteen or so years had passed.

One afternoon I was reading a new book that had just come out, on true Angelic encounters. One of the stories was about a woman who lived deep in the Florida everglades with her children. She had found herself in the midst of a desperate situation, and who, of all people should arrive, but a tall, handsome, black man in an all-white Texan style outfit; boots, hat, and all. He appeared miraculously from out of nowhere and disappeared into the same, after rescuing her family from a life and death situation.

"Hmm," I thought. "Why does that seem so familiar?" I put down the book and reflected on her description of the stranger. "Of course!" I exclaimed out loud. "Oh my goodness!" The remembrance, after all of those years, and the woman's description of what she believed was an Angelic encounter, made that night come alive once again and become even more meaningful than before.

Not only did the woman in this particular story describe his appearance and countenance exactly the same, but since reading that story I have heard several more accounts of an Angelic rescuer that fits this description to a tee. Because of miraculous interventions, everyone who had encountered him believed that he must have been an Angel.

That night after the tire was changed, I don't know what the two young men were thinking, but we were all quiet as they drove me to my house and dropped me off. Was I in danger that night? I have a strong feeling that I probably was. Did the appearance of that extraordinary stranger upset some planned or unplanned assault that might have taken place? Did his presence counteract an evilness that unknowingly was brewing around all of us that night? I suppose I'll never know, at least not while I'm here on this earth, but someday I hope to come face to face with this loving, mysterious stranger once again, and ask him.

CHAPTER 19

We've got to stop meeting like this

———— ∞∞∞ ————

W ᴇ ɴ ᴍ ʏ ᴅ ᴀ ᴜ ɢ ʜ ᴛ ᴇ ʀ J ᴇ ꜱ ꜱ ɪ ᴄ ᴀ ʟ ɪ ᴠ ᴇ ᴅ across from me for a year or so, on our little neighborhood street, she often slept with her front door open to let in fresh air through the screen door, as most of us did on summer nights. It was a small, peaceful community set apart in the country.

One night, my youngest daughter and I were awakened by screams. We both bolted out of the front door, and I was right behind Heather as we ran into Jessica's house. She had turned the light on by then, and was very much shaken. "What's wrong," we asked, "what happened?" To this day, twenty-six years later, she still vividly remembers that night.

She was sound asleep when something woke her. Through drowsy eyes, she saw three men standing near the couch, where she had fallen asleep. She automatically screamed even though she hoped that she might be dreaming. In seconds, she knew that she was wide awake, and thought that these strangers had come in through the door.

What was really odd, as she retells her account, as she gave out more screams, the three men never acknowledged her; they acted as if possibly they weren't even aware of her. They appeared to be concerned with, or observing something of interest, something that didn't have anything to do with my daughter, perhaps nothing to do with her world at all.

When Heather and I ran through the door Jessica frantically described what had happened, and waved her arms around the area in front of the couch several times, saying. "They were HERE, they were RIGHT HERE!" After Heather agreed to stay the night with her, we eventually all went back to bed thinking that tomorrow it would turn out to be just a bad dream.

She has told very few people. Like most of us who have had paranormal or unexplainable events, she keeps it in the back of her mind under, "Bizarre, but irrelevant in the real world." When she does talk about it, the thing that makes it so believable to me is that when she first screamed she thought that it might have come from not being fully awake, blurring reality with a dream. What sent her into terrified, continual screams was the fact that after she had sat up and was fully awake the dream did not end, the men were still there, and they did not leave.

When asked for details of the men, she said it is still hard to explain. They were ordinary in size, but it was as if they didn't quite fill the space like they should have. The room was dark, with only the light from the night, yet the visitors were lighter than the room, perhaps with what you could call a glow, but not glow-*ing*, per se; this included their clothing as well.

They didn't feel to her as though they were particularly Angelic, nor sinister. They mostly seemed as if they either weren't aware that they had intruded on her little corner of the world, or if they knew, that they were anything other than observers, if that much. She only screamed because she didn't know what else to do; the experience of finding three strangers, and ultimately unworldly sort of fellows standing in your home in the middle of the night was terrifying, but ultimately she did not feel personally threatened by them. She said they had disappeared as we were on our way across the street.

I don't know who these nocturnal visitors were, or what kind of phenomenon occurred, but I do know my daughter, and I believe her. To this day she says, "Nothing like this had ever happened before, and nothing like it has happened since.

When I was around eight years old my parents and I went to visit an older friend of my father. His friend was retired, and enjoyed making furniture in his home workshop. His wife, Anne, was a very nice lady whom my mother liked to visit, as well. Although we had visited many times before, throughout the years, I have always remembered a particular day when we went there, I believe for the last family visit.

The five of us were sitting in the living room of their two story home while the grownups talked, and then my mother, and her friend, and I went throughout the house, looking at, and admiring the pieces of furniture that her husband had made. The rooms were very pretty, and the house was older, even at that time, and included a large, enclosed sun room.

The three of us made our way out into the sunny room, where it was filled with vintage wicker furniture and plant stands. As we lingered there for a little while, I also couldn't help but notice the elderly woman who was sitting very quietly in a very old fashioned wheel chair.

After the little tour we went back into the living room, where I decided to go outside and check out the yard, and the interesting flower garden. After my little self-excursion, I came back inside by way of the sunroom at the back of the house.

The lady in the wheelchair was still sitting there, in the same place where I saw her the first time. Even though I tended to be very shy at times, sometimes the other person could be so nice and pleasant, that I would be comfortable to have a conversation. Especially with people who were older.

She was very kind, and had a nice smile, and it made me feel as though she enjoyed me being there and talking to her. I don't remember what I said, probably something about school, or my pets, just polite small talk, and unfortunately, I don't remember anything that she said, other than the fact that she was the mother of the lady whom we were visiting.

In a little while I went back into the house and sat down with my mother and our hostess. The men were busy in the workshop. Our hostess smiled at me, and asked me what I had been doing. "I walked around and looked at the flowers, and then I was talking to the lady on the porch," I replied.

They both were sort of looking at me, and then at each other. "*Oh, she said,*" (with almost a wink to my mother, as grownups often do to children when they think they are using an over active imagination,) "You were talking to a lady on the porch?" she repeated. She said it very nicely, but it was in a way that made me feel that perhaps the lady didn't usually talk to children, or I got something mixed up, or whatever....I didn't know which.

As the day progressed into evening, the men were on their own, and loving it, and we three girls decided to walk a few blocks to a little diner, and have a light meal. That is still a very vivid memory to me, as I enjoyed the walk, and the food, and the company.

Finally, it was getting late in the evening, and we said our goodbyes. As the years came and went, often I would think of the wonderful time we had with those friends, and the nice visit with the lady on the porch.

As I got older, one day the thought came to me, "Well, that was kind of strange, our hostess never went to check on her mother." And as I thought more seriously about that day, I remembered that not only did no one check on her, but she evidently never got any food, for it was never mentioned that maybe she might be hungry, too. She was never fed, or helped, or invited to be a part of our gathering. She was never mentioned, for that matter, in any way.

I started going over that day more and more, the older I got, and it just didn't make sense that a woman as nice as our hostess, or my own mother, would leave an elderly woman in another part of the house without checking on her, or seeing to her needs, or keeping her company. Nor did anyone ever mention that she might be tired and need to go to bed. As day had turned into night, I never saw hide nor hair of that woman the rest of the visit.

Finally, still curious years after the day that I had begun to wonder, I went to a foolproof and dependable source. I asked my mother if she had ever met Anne's mother, or if she was living with her when we would visit. I knew that my mother had a very good memory, even after she was elderly, she could recall times and people very well. She replied that she had never heard any mention about her friend's mother, and didn't know anything about her. She definitely had never seen, nor met her. (In my mind, I said to myself, "That solves one mystery.")

And even though they might have thought that I was just being a kid and making up a little tale at the time, they would have been astonished, no doubt, if they had known that the lady in the sunroom wasn't from my imagination. She was real, alright, but evidently I was the only one that day who had seen her, and who had talked with her. It turned out to be just a pleasant conversation between me and a sweet, motherly apparition, in the sunroom.

When I was a child, I had a beautiful and sweet aunt, named Nora. She was only nine years older than me, and she always loved to visit us when we lived just down the country road from grandma, or anywhere that we lived she would come and stay with us. I can still see her sweet smile, and hear her laughter.

I hold onto one precious memory, so well, that happened when I was about five. Nora, who would have been 14, cut one of my skirts into strips, so that it looked like a Hawaiian Hula skirt. When my mother walked out onto the porch, Nora told me to dance the hula for her, and they both laughed.

As so often in life, tragedy struck, when Nora was about sixteen. In grandma's house, the old back porch had a heavy cellar door that opened like the one in the Wizard of Oz. As Nora was walking down the cellar steps one day, the door fell shut, hitting her in the head and knocking her down the stairs.

Although initially she seemed to be okay, she soon started suffering from severe pain in her head and face. No one doctor or dentist seemed to know how to treat the pain, or what the outcome would be. Fate was so cruel that during this time, my beautiful, young aunt suffered in agony so terribly.

Finally, after a year or longer, it seemed as though good news came. At a Louisville Hospital the doctors said that the pain was from a damaged nerve in her face, and that it would just be a matter of clipping the nerve. To make this account as short as possible, for it hurts me to this day, Nora had the surgery, but she never regained consciousness.

On her death certificate it just states that she didn't respond from the anesthetic. In my heart I believe that in the operating room someone made a terrible mistake. But, in any case, it was done, and it broke something more than just our hearts when she died.

A few months later, one night, as I lay in bed, with the faint light of the night coming in through the windows of the house, I saw my mother walk up to my doorway. Just out of curiosity I asked her what she was doing standing there. In just a moment or so later, my actual mother walked into the hall, and into that space, where I first thought I saw her.

She asked me what I said. (I believe she knew that I had seen something, and I kind of believe that she may have seen the same thing.) I could now tell how more detailed my mother appeared, even in the shadows. As she had walked up to my doorway, the lighter, less detailed vision dropped softly down, and disappeared.

Around the same time, something very similar happened to my aunt Becky, who is only a year older than me, and who is Nora's baby sister.

One night she saw the wispy figure of someone standing close to her, in her bedroom. This vision also dropped down and disappeared. When she told her mother about it, grandma said not to be afraid, that it was just Nora watching over her.

It's not so hard to believe. In fact, for our family, it isn't hard at all. And I don't mind meeting like this, at all, when it is someone as pretty and sweet as Nora.

CHAPTER 20

Three pickles

───⊗⊗⊗───

I HAVE INCLUDED THIS STORY for my own amusement, and I hope it will be for yours as well. It is completely true, and as silly and trivial as it may sound to you, I believe that it happened for a reason. I haven't begun to figure out what all of those reasons of life are, but the exciting thing about the unknown is that I no longer feel that I have to understand it all; as long as God knows, and He does, then it is okay by me.

My story takes place on a sunny day in the late nineties. I had some free time before going to my job and decided to get something to eat. After buying hamburgers and a coke, I pulled my car into an empty area of the parking lot to enjoy the familiar view of the old store fronts and houses that made this part of town unique.

In Louisville, as well as many other American cities, we have a chain of little restaurants called, "White Castle." In 1921, Walt Anderson and Billy Ingram formed a partnership that resulted in their specialty; providing the everyday man with a nice cup of coffee, and exceptionally tasty hamburgers, for a phenomenally low price. Even now in 2017, their restaurants still offer a satisfying, inexpensive meal; all because two men put themselves in someone else's shoes.

Anyway, these were my thoughts, and the frame of mind that I was in as I sat enjoying the beautiful weather, and preparing to eat my meal. The other information that I will add is that always, since I was a young girl, when I was given a White Castle in its little box, the first thing I did was to check to see if the pickle was on it, because that was my favorite part. To this day, I always check my sandwich for the pickle, and then check the box to see if there might be an extra one that has fallen off, for every lucky once in a while you might get two. It's just one of those little quirky things that give me pleasure.

I went through my little ritual, and then started slowly eating. As I looked at the little white restaurant, I thought about Walt Anderson, and was appreciating the standard of quality that he had set for his food, and the consideration he had shown for the public. A soft, warm bun, a tasty piece of meat steamed with onions, and to top it off, a pickle slice.

I was totally in the moment of enjoyment and appreciation when I decided to save my extra hamburger for later. I looked down into the sack one more time before folding the top, and happened to glance at the empty box from the original hamburger. There was another large pickle slice.

"Hmm…" I said to myself. I had checked the box earlier, like always, and yet, there was a pickle that I had somehow missed. It didn't seem likely, but there it was. I gladly put it on the half that I was still eating. A bite or two later, and I knew that I had to get going to work. I looked down at the sack that I had not yet folded, and glanced down again at the two boxes. There in the same box was another big pickle slice! There wasn't any doubt this time, although there really wasn't any the first time; that pickle appeared out of nowhere.

When I told my granddaughter about the incident she wondered why God did it. I mulled that over. "I don't believe that God did it," I answered, "although He certainly can do anything that He wants. I have a feeling that it was most likely a playful Spirit, because I've had so many wonderful and unexplainable experiences lately. Perhaps that is the answer." "On second thought," I added, "Maybe it was Mr. Anderson. Maybe it was his way of thanking me for remembering him, and appreciating his efforts."

I don't know who put those pickles there, I only know what happened, it actually happened, and it makes me feel happy whenever I think about it.

An after note on this story happened several years ago. While out with my mother, we went to a White Castle. Since I didn't have one in the town where I lived, I was looking forward to my meal. It was slow that day, and we were the only ones in line as the cook prepared our burgers.

As I stood at the counter I once again thought of Walt Anderson and my pickle story. I was smiling to myself when I sat down, and thought, "Well, nothing like that can happen today because I don't have any hamburger boxes to find extra pickles in."

I removed the bun on the first hamburger, to check for the pickle, and there were three big pickle slices. I looked at the second burger and found three big pickle slices. Not having been there for a while, I asked my mother if they had started putting three pickles on their hamburgers. "No, I don't think," checking her meal, "I've only got one on each of mine." "That's funny," I replied, "because I wrote a story about three pickles in my book."

Was it just a coincidence? Skeptics would say that I'm reveling in a ridiculous, trivial, and impersonal run of wild imagination; and maybe they're right. But I believed then, and still do believe, that people like Mr. Anderson, who, by putting themselves in another person's place, choose to make the world just a little happier, and are anything but ridiculous, trivial, or impersonal; and perhaps the powers that be don't think they are either.

CHAPTER 21

Mad Dog

THERE ARE A FEW THINGS that have happened to me that I can honestly say are just too offbeat, or hard to believe, for even the most devoted or open-minded paranormal followers. "Three pickles," is one, "Unheard," is another, and "Mad Dog," tops the list.

My account takes place around 1985. It started when a woman that lived on the other side of our neighborhood acquired a dog that looked just like a wolf. It was blackish brown, and had an oddity of one brown eye, and the other blue. This dog felt no need to be friendly to anyone, had an inflexible aggressive personality, and had the suggestive name of "Mad Dog."

My first encounter with Mad Dog happened one day when I was walking home alone. I spied what looked like a collarless, bristled wolf slowly stalking me. I had nowhere to go, and tried to remember what I had heard about encountering strange dogs.

Was I supposed to avoid eye contact, or stare her down and show superiority? I couldn't remember. She crept behind me at a deliberate pace and then appeared to be closing in. I prepared myself for the worst but was so relieved when rescue came in the form of a large, friendly neighborhood dog that had taken a liking to me years before. As I petted and talked happily to my loyal friend, Mad Dog changed her stance. She was still distrustful, eyed us both suspiciously from a distance, but she wasn't going to bite me, I figured.

Before long, she became a most loving and loyal friend to my children and me, while remaining aloof and hostile to others. We knew that we were always safe when she was around, and she let everyone know it. Mad dog spent more time around, and in our home, than her own.

Late one bitterly cold night, my children and I drove home from an outing. As we walked to the front door I heard a familiar sound; the wooden door was open to the crawl space, and was banging back and forth in the snowy wind. I ran through the darkness and quickly shut and locked it.

Three days later my children were playing hockey on the frozen creek behind their friend's house, while I was at home. It was just getting dusk when suddenly I heard a sound that I knew all too well; water rushing through the water pipes. Because the pipes were close to the floor and had frozen, or out lasted their repairs so many times through the years that we lived there, and I was the one who had to fix them, I was well acquainted with the sound. We all were.

The way the water was rushing through those pipes I knew that it was a major break. I double checked the inside lines and then grabbed my tools and headed out the door to turn the water off the only way that I could, from the main meter. Since I had several lines that I had repaired with short pieces of hose, I decided to look under the crawl space first, and get an idea from which direction the water was coming.

I didn't have a flashlight as I stuck my head in, and it was taking my eyes a minute to adjust to the darkness, but I saw a channel of water that started from somewhere under the kitchen and ran off to the side.

On hands and knees, with my body half in the little doorway, unexpectedly I saw a movement from back in the darkness. Two eyes glowed as the faint light from the setting sun struck them, and they were quickly coming closer. I had swayed back in fright, but suddenly recognized the outline. It was Mad Dog, and she acted greatly relieved to see me. "Mad Dog," I sputtered. "What are you doing under there?"

I lovingly petted her, but then turned my attention back to my emergency. I could hardly comprehend; the familiar sound of the singing pipes was gone. All was strangely quiet. If there was one thing I knew, after many combined hours of lying on my back in freezing temperatures, broken water pipes didn't fix themselves, and a rushing source of water had to have an explanation.

With the small door opened to allow what light there was of the late evening sun to shine in, I crawled on my stomach the twenty five or so feet that it took to reach under the kitchen. The stream of water was now soaking in the dirt, but I saw what had obviously been the source, the outside water faucet. It had been moved from the yard to under the house a few years before because it had caused my lines to freeze one too many times. It was wet, and the ground around it was soaked from the short lived flood.

I went back into the house to consider what had just happened. I've never mistaken the dreadful sound of water rushing through the lines, and the proof was in the stream that was running toward me as I entered the crawlspace. My children were not home, and Mad Dog would barely tolerate (and only if we admonished her) when my neighbors approached our yard. And it's for sure that anyone would have had a dog fight on their hands if they had tried to crawl under our house. That was out of the question.

I thought more about Mad Dog. She must have been waiting for us and took shelter from the cold, the night that I ran over and locked the banging door. That meant that she had been trapped for three days. I know that dogs can be very smart, but is it possible that she could she have turned on that water faucet, and then turned it off as well?

That would have been quite a feat, and quite a masterful plan. Could there be another explanation, one that would have to be as equally amazing? Could it be that she had her own Guardian Angel that took pity on her and decided to help her out by getting my attention in a sure fire way?

Either explanation is incredible, but there has to be one. Mad Dog had certainly taken on the role of guardian by watching over us with her constant love, loyalty, and protection through those years, and I truly believe that *Someone* stepped in and offered her a helping hand.

CHAPTER 22

Now I've seen everything

—⊶⊷—

MY FRIEND CANDY HAD TOLD me an interesting story in the mid-sixties. She, and another friend were driving around Louisville one night, just talking and passing time, when they ended up in an area called Appliance Parkway, so named because it was the huge General Electric production site. Back then, other than a few quiet subdivisions and small, locally owned businesses, G.E. sat in what you could call semi-rural country. It was around one or two in the morning, a clear night, when my friend looked up and saw something really unbelievable. It was a huge craft of some type hovering over the General Electric plant.

They slowed the car down to barely rolling, but did not stop because they just could not figure out what they were seeing, and did not want to stay too long out in the dead of night, with whatever that thing was. My friend said that it was huge, dark, and was hovering silently over one of the main buildings. She thought that it was something like a triangle. It didn't fit the description of any earthly air-craft that we'd ever heard of.

Back then I could barely believe that life could exist other than on Earth, and yet I knew my friend, and I believed her. Small, classic saucers were, I suppose, more comprehensible to me, but if she said it was as large as the building that it was hovering over, then that's how it was, even if it didn't fit in with any other accounts that I had ever read.

We never talked about it too much after that, just every once in a while throughout the years, but when she would ask me if I remembered the U.F.O. that she saw, I would quickly answer, "Oh, yes, I sure do."

In fact, it was some thirty years later when a particular news story came out in the Louisville Courier Journal that I immediately thought of Candy. It seems that two policemen in a helicopter had both just witnessed, and reported seeing a huge, dark, silent craft of some type hovering over the General Electric plant a few nights before. Not only did the policemen in the air pursue this unidentified object, but there were other policemen in patrol cars who witnessed the same, as they all took off in pursuit of this craft. This first person, eye witness account from the Louisville Policemen has been told many times on television and radio programs since.

Candy had heard the story on a Louisville station also, and finally felt that she had the validation and verification of her own experience, since the accounts were so extraordinarily alike.

Later, we had more to talk about whenever we got on the subject of U.F.O.s and the paranormal, as the years passed, for we both seemed to be in the right places at the right or wrong times, depending on how you look at it, or purposely or inadvertently got caught in a wide hodgepodge of the mysterious; and I too had stories of my own that involved unidentified space crafts and anomalies.

In 1977, my husband was the evening desk clerk at an expensive, high-rise condominium complex. Sometimes I would take him to work at three in the afternoon and pick him up at eleven. This building sat on the edge of a very prestigious part of Louisville where the suburbs met the country, and it was easy to see the night sky.

One Friday evening, around ten o'clock, as my three children and I waited in the parking lot for him to get off work, a light in the sky caught my eye and I watched it, for no particular reason, as it slowly traveled from left to right. It just seemed like the type of white light that is on a small airplane when they are low in the sky. However, another white light caught my attention for it was coming from the right, and traveling in what appeared to be the same altitude, directly toward the first one. I started getting worried because if they were as close in proximity as they seemed they would surely hit head on if they continued.

When they got about two thumbs width from each other (from my view) I became aware of a red light of the same size descending toward the center of the others. When they reached about a half thumbs width they stopped in mid-air, forming a symmetrical triangular formation. I could hardly reason what I was seeing. For approximately three or four seconds they hung in the air motionless, and then simultaneously they shot upwards and backwards, and out of sight.

I heard someone exclaim, "Wow!" and realized that my eight and a half year old son who was sitting in the backseat must have seen the same thing that I had. I quickly turned to him. "Did you see that?" I exclaimed. He answered, "Yes," in a voice filled with excitement. It was easy to see that he was as amazed as I was.

A few years later, around 1983, my son and I were driving on a country road, late one summer's night. It was a starry, cloudless sky, and we had our windows down as we made our way home. I noticed a light of some sort beaming down into one of the fields that dotted the landscape. It was not in the field that lined this road, but seemed to be one or two farms away from us.

I slowed down and asked my son what kind of light he thought it was. We realized that this beam of light came all the way down to the ground, and saw that it went up into the night sky, and seemed to be coming from a star. It was not a brilliant light beam, somewhat dim and see-through, but it was strange and rather scary to see.

I can only describe it in layman's terms and sort of in the context of movies that I have seen. It was some type of star beam, whether it was man-made or natural, I don't know, but it appeared to be coming from an unimaginable distance. It did not waver, or change position, or intensity. It was slightly wider at the bottom, where it appeared to touch the field.

Suddenly I had the strangest feeling, almost as if we were being watched, or we weren't alone, and I didn't want to find out just then what that light was all about. I wanted to get home. I don't mind to admit that it started feeling very scary, creeping along that quiet, deserted country road and watching that eerie beam. "The X-Files" hadn't yet aired, but if it had, I would have sworn that I had just driven into one of its episodes.

Surely it was going to be all over the news; I would read about it then. Unfortunately, if anyone else saw it, they weren't talking, and there never was a word of it mentioned in the news; but of course back then things like that rarely were.

I experienced one other incident that I always think back on and wonder about. It was approximately late 1982. My husband, children, and I had just returned from a school program, and it was around 9:30. The four of us sat in the yard for a while admiring the starry sky. It was another clear night and the night sky was brilliant in the rural setting. In a while my husband and two daughters went inside but my son and I continued to search the sky for constellations and interesting celestial bodies.

I was facing north-west as I let my eyes wander high into the heavens. My eyes rested on what looked like a distant star for it was very small compared to some of the others, and I just happened to catch sight of a pin-point sized red dot moving toward it.

No sooner had it disappeared but another red dot came into view and disappeared into the light as well. Red dots of light were now entering from both sides as well as from the top and the bottom. They were moving in what I would say a steady pattern, and were traveling rather slowly, not like meteors that sail into view in an instant and then are gone; and they didn't change size, brilliance, or color. I got the impression that they were solid and controlled.

I stopped counting at seventeen, and then called my son over and showed him where to look. Several more came into view as we watched that star, or planet, or whatever it was. I know that it sounds like a scene out of "Star Wars," but that's exactly what it reminded me of; a group of manned space crafts coming into the port of a huge space station after a day's maneuvers. Needless to say, we never heard about that on the news either.

Around 2003, I reported all three sightings to Peter Davenport's website, dedicated to the investigation of U.F.O. sightings. These accounts still intrigue me to this day, and will forever be framed in my memory, but for some reason, an account that seems to linger and intrigue me the most came from a neighbor and good friend of 23 years.

Pop, as everyone in the neighborhood called him, was a retired electrician who was already in his early seventies when we moved next door. He had a grown son who was a respected State Policeman, a grandson who was stationed aboard a nuclear submarine in the South Pole, and was an Elder in his church. He was as solid and sound as anyone I ever knew, and more than normal.

On hot summer nights he would often sit on his porch swing, and relax into the wee hours, with the crickets and the stars. My children and I passed a lot of time on that porch with him. Pop was intelligent, interesting, and just plain good company. One night, after getting on the subject of space and all its amazements, he told me this account of something that had happened in the early 1970's. It was then about 1996.

He was sitting on his porch late one night, taking in a full moon and thousands of stars in the country sky. He became aware that the sky seemed a little dimmer somehow, and he looked out further to see what was going on. He couldn't see any particular thing in the sky, and yet some of the stars seemed to be blotted out, as though being devoured by an invisible entity. Silently, the moon and all surrounding objects disappeared in darkness.

Pop realized, though it seemed impossible, that some dark, almost stealth object was passing between him and the celestial bodies, far above from where he sat watching. Whatever it was, in his judgment, was unbelievably huge, traveling in a steady and slow silence. He watched attentively as the moon and areas of surrounding starlight temporarily disappeared, and then moments later came back into view.

I had never heard of anything like this, except in the case of my friend Candy. Until then, I was unaware of any other UFO sightings that had ever been larger than the ordinary flying saucers that you generally heard about in those days. But now, in 2016, I have heard plenty about the large, dark, triangular ships, and otherwise shaped, that so many people have sighted, and I believe, and have no doubt that this was what Pop saw.

Some of you say, "Joy is greater than sorrow,"
and others say, "Nay, sorrow is the greater."
But I say unto you, they are inseparable.3

The Prophet; Khalil Gibran

CHAPTER 23

My Son Chris

—⚬⚬⚬—

IN EARLY 1993, I STARTED experiencing many troubling dreams. They were always centered on black animals, or black objects, and the animals were either dying, or dead. There would be a variety of people changing from dream to dream, but my son was always present, usually as a little boy.

Long before this time, I had begun noticing that whenever I had repetitive, morbid dreams something terrible would happen. It didn't take many of these foreboding dreams before I began to worry. Two new nightmares added to the suspicion that these were no ordinary, arbitrary dreams, but could possibly hold forewarning significance. Both were about weddings.

In each dream someone that I knew would be getting married. I would be excited and happy to be taking part of the festivities but my happiness would soon turn to bewildered sadness; for in the first dream, to my dread, those in the bridal party were all in long, black dresses. In the second, everyone around me was dressed in beautiful white gowns. I excitedly looked down to see what I was wearing, but was horrified to see that I was dressed in a long black dress and veil.

The many dreams I had during this time gave me cause for further worry. My father, who was deceased, was in several of them. After one particular dream, I felt certain that he was trying to tell me something:

I was standing in the farmhouse that belonged to my fathers' sister. As I looked out of the window I saw my father standing by a coffin, and that he was crying. (I thought to myself that my mother must have died, even though in real life he was the one who was dead), but then I realized that my mother was standing next to him, and crying also. Suddenly my dad was standing across the room from me and he was trying to tell me something, (it was as if his heart were breaking.) I tried so hard, but I couldn't hear or understand what he was saying.

The dream ended there, and my apprehension grew.

Another dream concerning my son involved me going to visit him at his apartment:

As I was cutting across the yard on my way to his apartment door, a man, who was leaning against a tree, told me that he was sorry that he got carried away, and he would help straighten things up. As I looked at him closely, trying to figure out what he meant, I realized that he was quite a bit older than my son and his friends, and that he was dressed in a way that made me wonder how he could know Chris. Something about him gave me cause for alarm.

As I approached the sidewalk I noticed that a crowd had gathered around the door. A nurse walked out and told me that Chris was sick; he would be okay, but that I couldn't go in just now. I told her that he was my son, and I pushed my way through all of the people. He was unconscious, and I told someone to call 911. As I held him in my arms, I could see the strands of color through his hair and the features on his face so clearly, as though I were really holding him.

It seemed too real to be a dream. (The man in the dream turned out to be an inmate in the jail where my son would be held six or seven months later. His appearance seemed threatening at first, but he turned out to be a kind person.)

In another dream I was with my youngest daughter. We were stranded, and trying to find a ride home, when a lady that my daughter had met a few times where she worked invited us to ride with her. A crowd soon gathered around her car, and I realized that they were angry.

I could feel the hate aimed toward my daughter and I, and I couldn't understand why. In the center front of the crowd, set off a little from the others, I saw a young man with long dark hair. He didn't seem to be angry, but just looking at us as though in deep thought. The crowd seemed to loom closer and closer, and I cried out in desperation, "Why do you hate us? You don't even know us." It was a chilling dream.

The first time that I actually saw the lady in my dream was in a court-room, months later. Her son, while on a camping trip, had been shot by a young friend that had become psychotic after taking LSD. I had never met him, but I realized that the dark haired boy in my dream was her son.

None of these dreams had any singular meaning at the time, and I couldn't understand their relation until months later. When I had this next dream, my uncle Ray was ill with cancer:

I was driving along a country road in heavily wooded mountains. I saw a large group of people standing along the edge of the road and real-ized that many of them were family members. As I got out of my car and approached them I saw that they were looking down into a grassy, wooded ravine. I begin to worry that this might be a funeral procession, and I looked around for my uncle. I was relieved to see that he was still alive, but it occurred to me that my son wasn't there. I felt very uneasy. I noticed that yellow tape was roping off a large area.

When I thought about that dream it hadn't occurred to me that it was yellow Police tape that I saw in the woods. Not until I just happened to see some roping off an area at a gas station, the first day that I drove to see my son who was being held in a rural, county jail. Sad, and deep in shock,

I realized just how prophetic that dream had been. Police tape and mountainous woods. It was something that should happen only in dreams, and those dreams are not supposed to come true!

During this time while I was experiencing fears of impending peril concerning my son, I started having them for my youngest daughter as well. Dreams once again were the catalyst. In these dreams, the surroundings might change, but the format would always be the same:

I would start searching for my daughter because I sensed that something was wrong, but by the time that I found her it would be too late. Someone would have beaten her to death.

These were horrible dreams that would haunt me for days. In this case, because they were so specific, I immediately started warning her to be extra careful. She lived alone at the time and worked nights, and I was very concerned. In the beginning she tried to act nonchalant and I felt that she might not be taking my warnings seriously enough, but I found out later that she had actually taken them more seriously than I thought.

Right after my son was arrested, she came home one night, to find that someone had tried to force their way in. They had made a split in the heavy door jam, but were not able to damage the dead bolt lock. We'll never know who, or what the real motive or intention of the "would be intruder" was, but the final dream in that series that occurred right before the attempted break-in was me finding my daughter beaten to death, in her bathroom.

The fear and worry of my daughter being harmed vanished with the last foreboding dream. I believe that the person or persons who tried to intrude into her home had a change of heart for some unknown reason. When the dreams first started I literally prayed day and night for Gods' protection of her, and that His angels would be around her constantly. When it was over with, I thanked God over and over for the forewarning dreams, and the chance to flood her with prayer and protection. I believe that it saved her life.

I don't understand why, but this was not to be for my son, and there was no happy ending. Why I couldn't act on my son's behalf, I do not know. I was so perplexed by the dreams concerning him, and what it all could mean, that I was paralyzed. Say too little or say too much; I ended up not saying anything at all.

When we would visit each other Chris seemed like his regular self and nothing in his behavior gave me cause for alarm. I had never had problems with Chris being temperamental or unreasonable, from the time he was little. I didn't ever have to worry that he would be anything but kind and calm in any situation. He had always been an easy going kid, one that was compassionate and caring to animals and children alike, particularly whenever he thought that I or his sisters were sad. We all loved being around him.

When I realized that he smoked marijuana and drank occasionally, he would always assure me that he wasn't doing it too much, and that he knew he should quit. He would say it in such a sensible way that I had hopes of him doing just that. His sisters and I were concerned about this, and emphasized that it wasn't the best way to deal with life, or have a good time, but he would smile good-naturedly and tell us not to worry about him, that he'd be okay. I didn't know until much later how serious his problems with addictions had become, or that he had told friends he didn't want to add any more worry to my life by talking about it to me.

One afternoon when he came home to take his sister and her daughter to the eye doctor, he removed a handgun from his truck; careful to keep his two year old niece safely out of its reach. I was very concerned that he had started carrying a handgun, and that he thought he needed one for protection.

On his days off from work he enjoyed rock rappelling and camping in the mountains with his friends. A lot of people took guns to the mountains to target practice, but I was leery of handguns, and told him that it was not a good idea to carry one. My father had taken Chris hunting since he was small so I could understand him taking a rifle, but handguns were different, and I was afraid that someone would accidentally shoot Chris.

Along with the odd dreams of animals, and subsequently the others that I recounted, I began having a reoccurring dream:

My mother and I were always in a medical facility. It would be a hospital lobby or some type of doctor's office. It was always just a little different in the layout but the feeling was always the same. I was the patient, but it didn't seem to be for surgery or something that I might not survive, at least I didn't think so. I would be waiting to find out what was going on. The main story line of the dreams was that I would be talking to a doctor and I would be terribly upset; inconsolable, in fact. My mother would be next to me, and she would be comforting me, and telling the doctor how upset I was, and then she would say, "Someone knows more about this than they are letting on. There is something not right about this whole thing, and I am going to get to the bottom of it."

A few months later my son was arrested, and held in jail awaiting trial. Nothing in life had prepared me for the grief and inconsolable pain that I felt for my son and the families that were drawn into this real life drama. I felt as though I were hanging by a thread.

One day, I felt that I just could not go on. I couldn't sleep, I couldn't think, I couldn't even catch my breath. I drove to my doctor's office and as soon as I got there I called my mother and asked her if she could come. My doctor, who knew my entire family, took his time to be encouraging and comforting. He and my mother were talking about the strain that

we were all under. My mother started talking about the unusual circumstances and the strangeness of the events that had occurred.

In my distraught frame of mind it was many months after that day in
my doctor's office that I recalled the dreams, for I had pushed everything
but the most crucial to the back of my mind. They had come true, or
perhaps, I should say that for some reason I had picked up precognitive
information that was certainly to be, evidently was inevitable, and was
critical enough to warrant forewarning.

It wasn't the first time that my dreams had been prophetic, and it
wouldn't be the last, but the difference now is that I have come to take
any, and all warnings very seriously, and it has made the difference in so
many instances concerning my family and me. I immediately start praying
in whatever direction, or for the person that the feelings seem to involve.
I tell the persons to be extra careful, or to watch out for certain signs. If I
don't know who or what it involves, I pray all the harder.

The overwhelming sadness and guilt that I live with every day is that I
could not prevent the tragedy that occurred to, and because of my son. It
was Chris that had taken the LSD on that camping trip, and it was he who
had shot his friend in a hallucinatory psychosis. His own twenty-two year
old life was irreparably altered, and the life of a young man, only twenty
years old, would end in a senseless and untimely death.

This is the reason that I have written this chapter. I have spent many
years questioning why I had apparent warnings, and yet was not given
enough information to be of use. I have strained to understand why I
didn't know what to do, or, if in fact there was anything that I was supposed to, or could have done. I cried out to God, "What good are premonitions if you can't do something to avert the tragedy into which you are
drawn?" Were dreams involving the future meant to be a blessing, or to
just leave you in a painful quandary of what-if?

I offer our story and our most personal trials for this reason, to encourage and warn you to take those "odd" feelings, intuitions, and premonitions seriously. For my son, I had pondered and reasoned out too many warnings; I had dismissed them for fear of weighing him down, or sounding foolish, or over paranoid.

If only I could just go back there would be so many things that I would have done differently. I would not have expected him to work out his addiction problems alone, perhaps preventing that heartbreaking and tragic outcome. I wouldn't have just smiled patiently and hoped for the best. I would have acted when I was besieged with urges instead of counting the cost of being wrong and sounding foolish.

I would have taken more time with this precious son of mine to know how worried he was, or how inadequate he felt. I would have recognized the terrible guilt he carried in his heart for never being able to take care of me and his sisters. I would have known that his smile hid a heart that was filled with pain, and in his mind, forever broken. I would have recognized that those same shadows of smiles were often on the faces of my daughters.

He was only twenty-two, and I had made the mistake of thinking that he was all grown up and no longer needed anyone to show him the way. I was so naive to think that by believing everything was alright in his world, that it would make it so. But I was wrong!

I have come to believe that some things are inevitable, and most are meant to play out for reasons that we don't understand; that sometimes the forces of Heaven must look on with wounded hearts, powerless to prevent the consequences of choices that we have made.

I believe that my father, yes, and even the Angels in Heaven were intensely caught up in the coming tragedy. Was it the inevitable that they were preparing me for? Were they letting me know that while they were unable to step in and alter the future, that they were ever at hand to aid and support?

I am convinced that I could not have endured without the kindnesses or sweet spirit of those unseen visitors that touched my life so many times, during this crucial and devastating time, and from that day on. I have relied heavily on this reassurance that I wasn't alone, and many, many times just to get myself out of bed in the morning, and back again at night.

I was able to comfort and console my son with these accounts, and to give him hope that all was not in vain, or without hope. I truly felt that these unseen presences were as real and loving as any earthly being, and as unfathomable as it seems, had an intense interest in me and my family.

I think that prayers from a broken heart go a long way and may be the very thing that keeps this world turning and supplied with compassion and love. Like casting bread upon the water, we must wait with faith and hope for the outcome

CHAPTER 24

Sarah and Sean

—∞∞∞—

MY MOTHER HAS ALWAYS EXPERIENCED premonitions and prophetic dreams, and if she told me to avoid a certain area, or had a 'feeling' that I shouldn't do something, then I knew not to. As it turns out, this ability has come not only to me, but my children as well.

I was just getting to know Sarah, a policewoman, that my daughter is especially close to, and her husband, Sean, when I had a vivid dream about them. In my dream I walked into my daughter's kitchen and saw Sean standing by the sink. I couldn't understand then, but he seemed troubled, and I was aware of several guns on the counter. I then found myself out by the barn and looking at the barn cats running in the field. They were all black, with just a little muted color instead of light tan's and grays, like in reality. As I looked at them I realized that now they weren't cats at all, but rabbits. Once again I was in the house, and a large number of Heather's friends and acquaintances were standing in a large group. Sarah was on the outside, as if trying to see what was happening in the center of the crowd. The dream ended there.

Since I have numerous dreams every night and the content is as varied as it can get, I don't automatically tell everything that I have dreamed, or expect that it will come to pass. I assumed that it was most likely a harmless dream and nothing to worry my daughter about.

However, the next time that I saw her, she related a dream to me that she had a few nights before. In the dream, she was standing in her back yard, when she saw Sarah and Sean's dogs chasing goats across her property. It was very strange to her for instead of their usual colors, the dogs, just like those strange goats, were all black. That's when she looked out across her fields and was stunned to see that they had been covered over in pitch black asphalt. It was a foreboding and eerie sight.

She had remembered when I told her about the significance of black animals or objects in my dreams, which almost always foretold of death or disaster, and she wondered what it could mean. It was only a few days after when we got our answer. Sarah's young husband committed suicide. He had left a note for his wife and children, and then went out into a wooded area where someone other than his wife would find his body, and shot himself.

They seemed to have been a couple that most everyone envied for it was obvious that they were still very much in love after seven years of marriage, doting on each other constantly. It was a tragedy that one expected, or could comprehend.

I thought back to the dreams that my daughter and I had. It still amazes me when things like this happen, but it no longer surprises me. I still struggle with the guilt and sadness of not being able to intervene before a tragedy occurs. This is why, when a story follows through with, if not a happy ending, but at least some communion of earth and Heaven, then I feel so thankful to God.

A few months after the funeral, Sarah called. It was to return the call I made to the police department the night before, checking to see if my daughter was on duty that night. I had been concerned for Sarah, but did not call her directly. I thought she needed time to heal with her family and close friends, and I didn't want to intrude.

When the phone rang that morning, Sarah asked me if we could talk. "Of course," I answered. She wanted to ask what I thought about life after death, and if I thought Sean might still be close by and aware of what was going on. She knew about the dreams of her and Sean.

I sat down and thought about the night, a few weeks before, when I was speaking to Sean in my heart. I told him how sorry I was that I hadn't known that he was contemplating suicide, and that I wish I had been able to help. It was such a tragedy for a wonderful person like Sean to come to that lonely and desperate place so early in life, in despair with the belief that there was no other way out.

I have never thought of myself as a medium, and still don't, but I told Sean that if there was anything that he wanted me to tell Sarah then I would try really hard to listen to him. I closed my eyes and cleared my mind. Immediately the word "Believe" came to my mind, with little words like "joy and peace, faith and hope," and various other words of encouragement and spirituality encircling it. The image of Snoopy, sitting in a red wagon, also came to me.

I made a serious mistake that I think others may make when they are new to this process. I considered the content, and then dismissed some of it because I thought that it just didn't sound like something Sean would say. I second guessed myself and feared that this may have just been my imagination giving way to wanting to comfort Sarah. I hope I never make that mistake again.

On the phone Sarah talked about her feelings and her uncertainties about the afterlife and the existence of God. She wanted to believe that there was a Heaven and that Sean was still alive somewhere, and that he could still be around her. She wanted to believe that he was alright. "Did you know that my nickname for him was 'rabbit'? She asked. I thought of the dream and the field full of rabbits. "No, I never knew that,' I answered.

Still feeling a little shy and unworthy, I told her about the heartfelt intent I had made to Sean and the vision of the word "BELIEVE." I tried to comfort her with my own beliefs and experiences that have led me to feel assured that God not only exists, but that we are precious to Him, that life goes on, and we can continue to learn the things that will bring us ultimately to perfect harmony and happiness with Him.

She thoughtfully contemplated each thing that I said. After a deep silence, she told me that she had thought of calling many times before, but now the time just seemed right, and now she understood why. She told me that she had bought some large postcards after Sean's death. She had been sadly wandering around a store when she saw them. She wanted to hang them as pictures in an arrangement because they were so pretty, and spoke to her heart.

In the center of each card was a word in bold print, with little words all around them. "Words like joy, and peace, faith and hope, and a bunch of other ones." she said. (I had not mentioned all of the little words around the vision that I had.) I felt a stab of guilt for not giving the message exactly as I had seen it. I felt as if I had let Sean down.

I hadn't totally failed though for Sarah told me that one of the cards had the word 'BELIEVE' on it. She said that at the time, because of her own doubts, she didn't know why she had even bought that one. At that point we were both quietly contemplating the significance of the cards, and our conversation. She told me that she had forgotten about them, still in the little bag in the back seat of her car, and asked me if she could call me again. I assured her that she could call me anytime that she wanted to.

A few days later I got a call from her, "I couldn't wait to look at those cards after we talked," she said. "When I put the bag in the front seat and opened it, the cards were still stacked neatly on top of each other. The card on the top, with the word in bold print was, "BELIEVE." We both said that we had goosebumps. She started crying softly. Rather gingerly, I asked, "Does Snoopy, sitting in a red wagon mean anything to you?" She answered, "It was one of Sean's favorite stories that he always told me about how he would pull his dog around in his wagon."

"What do you think it all means?" she asked. We talked for quite a while about life, and the bonds of love, and God's role in everything we do. Two things come to mind when I think of this experience. I think Sarah needed to know that Sean was still a part of her life and that he was very aware and connected to this earthly plane.

I do believe that he was with her the day that she picked out the postcards and that this was his way of letting her know. And I also believe that it is important to God that we have support and strengthening in our days of unfathomable grief, when doubt can cause despair to overtake us, and faith and hope cease to exist. Sean would have understood that all too well, and I believe that he used love and determination to send help to Sarah, as he communicated it to me.

I BELIEVE that it is truly amazing when help comes in unexpected and miraculous ways.

CHAPTER 25

The Music Box

———⊶⊷———

My father was the strength of our family when I was growing up, and my morning sun. I knew that life would go on and problems always work out because daddy was in the world. It was as though his patience held the very foundations of the universe together, and his smile warmed the earth. When he died, I felt as though the world dropped out from under my feet and I was suspended over an abyss, dazed and uncertain of how I could go on.

When a tragedy of so different a scenario struck my family, five years later, it was just too much. I had lost my beloved father, and now my twenty-two year old son was in a life and death situation that a mother could never imagine in her wildest nightmare.

I began to question my every thought and action of the past. While trying to piece together the life of my son, and my two daughters, in my mind, I had to reflect on my own, as well. So many of those years that we struggled were hard to remember. It was as though, at times, each of us were missing. Memories came to me that made me wonder how we managed at all.

There were good times, for sure. We laughed a lot, and spent a lot of time together, but the most painful and destructive events loomed over us, and we all seemed unable to do anything about them but hide from, or ignore them. Of course, that's all children can do, but what about me?

I had developed a pattern of dealing with life's problems by hiding from the reality, myself.

In my inability to deal with difficulties, I had inadvertently left so much for my children to deal with. "Oh no," I cried out loud to God, as all of those painful revelations came to the surface of my mind. How many times I had failed those little ones so cruelly. I hadn't meant to. I hadn't ever wanted anything or anyone to ever hurt them, or cause them to want for anything.

The more I studied our lives in an attempt to understand why my son had turned to alcohol and drugs, the deeper the pool of hardship and isolation within each family member became clear. It was a pool that I felt like drowning myself in.

These new revelations, adding to the despair and sadness that now enveloped my son, as well as my entire family, sent me into a passion of crying and self-hated until one night I literally crumpled to the floor. I could do nothing but cry out to my father. "How could you still love me after the terrible choices that I have made? I've made so many stupid and selfish mistakes that I can't even bear to think of them. I wouldn't blame you if you hated me for the times that my children were so unhappy, and I was so inadequate. You were so good, and worked so hard to give me everything that I needed and to always be there for me, and I let you and everyone down! How could I have done that?" My life seemed like a pointless, wasted effort! I didn't deserve to live.

Just then I heard music playing, and it played for quite a moment. It was so crystal clear that it startled me, and I froze for a moment. "Where is that music coming from?" I whispered to myself, tears still running down my face. The little chimes sounded familiar. "The music box! Where is it?" I whispered.

A few months before, my mother had sent me home with a brass music box that consisted of a rowboat with a brass fisherman made of wire, wearing a hat, and holding a fishing pole. I had put it up, out of the way where it would be safe until I moved, until it had a permanent place. That had been a couple of months before and I had forgotten all about it.

It had belonged to my father, and had sat on his dresser. He loved to fish, and the boat looked like the kind that I had seen him in all of his life. I had wound the music box a few times after daddy died, and watched as the brass boat would go around on the frame underneath. In order to play it had to turn, boat and all. I looked around the living room from where I sat, and located it on top of a tall cabinet. It hadn't been wound in months.

Sitting in its place, all by itself, I knew that it had had plenty of opportunity to 'unwind', if that had been the case. I pushed on the boat to see if it was still wound and had a few extra notes in it, but no, I had to force it to play one more note. I had used the tight drawer in that cabinet often and it would have been shaken and jolted to play, if it had been wound still. I put my hand over my mouth in bewilderment, fresh tears running down my face. "Daddy, is that you?" I whispered. "Are you really here with me?"

I truly felt that he had been listening to everything that I had said that night, and the many nights since his death. He had never deserted me or let me down, or anyone else for that matter, while he had walked on this earth, and I guess it just wasn't too incredulous that he would still be close by and connected to the ones he loved.

There wasn't a mechanical or rational reason for that music box to start playing just then, and to some, it is impossible. However, I really do believe that with God, ALL things are possible, even the simplest things that some people call 'unbelievable'.

The story of my father's music box doesn't end here, however, for I wasn't through with my sorrow, and daddy evidently wasn't through with me.

My dad and me. He was the kindest, most loving
person that I have ever known.

CHAPTER 26

Music Box (two)

⸺❈⸺

MY YOUNGEST DAUGHTER HAS BEEN a dispatcher and clerk for a Police Department since 1995. While visiting her one night at her work, a man came up to the desk and asked if he could see his daughter. She was being held for theft, and he was to meet with the detective who was holding her. It seems that she worked for a fast food restaurant and had evidently taken money from her cash register. I believe that she was sixteen.

Her father was a very polite and well-dressed man who was obviously angry at having to pick his daughter up from a police station. He looked at me and shook his head as if to say that he was embarrassed and upset. In a few minutes he was shown into a conference room, and I continued my visit.

It was dark by the time that I walked out into the parking lot. The man and his daughter were standing by the curb. She was crying, and he was still angry by the look of his body language. I got the feeling that he had half a mind to throw up his hands and just leave her standing there.

I walked on to my car, which was parked several yards away, and got in. I felt sorry for both of them, having been a daughter and parent myself. I didn't want to make things worse by intruding into their private business but I felt compelled not to leave.

Hesitantly, I got out of my car and walked over to them. As gently as I could, I explained that I didn't mean to intrude. "You see," I said, to the father, "I have a son in prison, and I always felt that if I could just bring him home one more time that maybe I could make everything alright."

"Just don't give up on her," I said gently, fairly sure of the myriad worries and fears that he must have been experiencing. Fresh tears ran down the girl's face as she looked for a sign that her father could forgive her.

His tense shoulders dropped visibly and it seemed as if he were finally able to take a slow, deep breath. With tears in his eyes, he said, "You don't know how much I needed to hear that. Thank-you for caring." Gazing at his daughter, who looked so young and vulnerable, he smiled reassuringly.

I have told this account for a specific reason, for it plays an important role in the second part of "The Music box."

When I was preparing to move, I packed my most valuable possessions carefully. I took wads of newspaper and tightly secured the fragile, or breakable. My father's music box was one of them. I put it in a plastic tub and padded it so that nothing on it could move, and therefore not get bent out of shape. I had moved this tub from the kitchen, into the living room, and to various parts of the room while I packed, and moved items, and pieces of furniture over several weeks.

One day while still packing and rearranging things, it happened that my frame of mind, being fragile itself, became very sad and disheartened. For some reason, the couple at the police station crossed my mind, and I hoped that they were able to find a happy solution to their problems.

I thought about how wonderful it would be if I could call my dad once again, knowing that he would always come, and how comforting that would be. Tears that were so easily found since the arrest of my son came running down, and I felt so alone. "If only I could see your face one more time, or hear your voice," I whispered to my dad, always hoping that he was somewhere close.

As I moved boxes and tubs closer to the front door, crying all the while, I was filled with heartache over losing him. "If only I could hear your voice once more," I said.

Clear as a bell, musical notes danced in my ears. They surprised and caught me off guard, just like the first time that I heard them from on top of the cabinet. I realized that the music box was in the container in front of my feet. When I took off the lid, there it was, tightly packed in its restraints. Again, I had to force the boat to turn in order to get one more note to play. I dropped to my knees, and looked at the little brass boat.

It wasn't much bigger than six or so inches, but it had meant a lot to both of us. It was heart breaking when daddy had to give up all of the independent things that he loved, one by one, due to his Alzheimer's. He must have looked at that little boat and the happy fisherman in it and wished a hundred times that he could once again enjoy those simple plea-sures. The only consolation that I could find in his death was the assur-ance that he was free of that terrible illness.

When that music filled the air on those two occasions, I could feel my father reaching out in the same comforting and loving way that he had all of my life, and I cried tears of thankfulness. God had allowed me to be acknowledged in some very 'special ways,' and most of all, I could feel assured that daddy was well and safe, and being taken care of too!

CHAPTER 27

Our Lady of Lights

———— ∞∞∞ ————

THERE HAVE BEEN EVENTS IN my life that have brought comfort in the midst of sadness and hope among an overload of troubles. I have been shown kindness and mercy when I felt that I just could not go on, and it is these moments that I draw upon to give me the courage and strength to face each new day.

I am thankful for each and every blessing that has been shown me, but there is one moment, one divine blessing that has lifted and preserved me like no other, and it is this that I fix my heart and compass on as I travel on this journey called life.

In 1998, I had taken up sewing again, and started spending time in the craft and material section of a store that was close to my job. I began having casual conversations with one worker who was there most of the time when I shopped. When she mentioned that she was going to a prayer meeting on her day off, I asked her where it was. It was a little Catholic church, about an hours' drive from the store, where she and a regular group went once a month to pray for the world. She told me that they had seen many miracles there, including visions of Our Lady, (Jesus' mother), and other Saints.

This was so wondrous to hear, and I was thankful for having met Anna. She went on to tell me that in August she and her group were going to another church, St. Joseph's, in Norwood, Ohio, because Our Lady had announced that she would come once a year in August, for seven years. Each consecutive year the crowds grew larger as the word spread of her promise, and each year on August thirty-first, at midnight, she would reveal her presence by a brilliant display of lights.

I had heard of miraculous things like this happening in the past but I did not know that something like this could still happen, and that I could be a witness to it. I was so excited, and yet I truly could not fathom that an extraordinary thing like this would come about.

The morning of Our Lady's promise came, and my cousin and I packed lawn chairs and a picnic basket, like Anna had suggested, and started off. We arrived at the huge, beautiful church that had once been a monastery, and marveled at its serene location on several acres of a groomed grassy hill in the center of town. Since it was still early in the day we were able to find a location about twenty or so feet to the right side of the stairs and doorway where Father Smith would be leading the Rosary and other special prayers all day, and into the night.

There were pieces of paper on a table for anyone who wished to write prayer requests. Due to the number of people that would be attending they could not be personally read, but would all be collectively prayed over during the day. I wrote down a cousin's husband with Multiple Sclerosis, and a neighbor, who had asked that her daughter be remembered, who had liver cancer, and then I poured out the heartache so painful, and yet so dear to me, that of my son, who was in prison. In just a few, simple words, I cried out for the child that I loved with all of my heart and anguished for with all of my sorrow.

We spent the day in prayer and taking walks through the church that was filled with beautiful crucifixes, paintings, and statues. There were photographs of previous years where dazzling lights were caught flashing through the crowds. I was amazed at the ribbons of rainbow lights that were caught on film and it was really hard for me to grasp what had happened, and what might happen tonight, but a feeling of sweetness and awe had fallen over me as I went through the day and I felt like a child in anticipation of a surprise.

As each hour passed in prayer and conversation I couldn't understand how I could be so blessed to be here. Among news teams, priests and nuns, spectators of all types, I was here, awaiting the arrival of Our Lady, the mother of Jesus. I had one foot on the ground, and the other in joyful and mystified bliss at this expectation.

I had always loved Mary but I knew that I did not say my rosary as often as I should, and I was not worthy of such a visit; did I even deserve to be in this crowd? My worry was soon addressed and relieved. Before each of the Rosaries, Father Smith would talk to the audience, which at sunset, had grown to about five thousand people. During one occasion he told us that this was a very special occasion for all of us were here because we had been personally invited by Our Lady. Tears of gratitude and joy to this most Holy Heavenly visitor ran down my face as I knelt and prayed with the crowd.

I meditated on the Angelic vision I had seen years earlier, and the times that unseen hands and voices had saved me and my family from harm. I remembered the days and nights of struggles that we had gone through, and how a real and loving presence of God had been my consolation and refuge. I had cried out to Mary, Jesus' mother, so many times in fear and desperation for my son whose life literally was hanging in the balance of the courts, and I had sought peace and rest at the feet of the most innocent and most compassionate refuge of all, Jesus of Nazareth, the Son of God. As the day turned to night, I awaited yet another sign that God was, and always will be the answer, and it was ecstasy just to be there.

As Father Smith got ready to lead the last Rosary he most reverently reminded us that Our Lady would be coming at midnight, as she promised, and that this last Rosary would be a very special one. I listened intently as he spoke so tenderly to the crowd. "This last Rosary will be a very special Rosary," he said again. It will be said for those who cannot be with us tonight, those who are in prison." An uncontrollable sob escaped from my throat, in total surprise, and in most humble gratitude a flood of tears streamed down my face, and I cried all through that Rosary. It had been my deepest prayer, my deepest hurt that my son could not be here, and for the most fearful circumstance of his life at this moment.

I thanked our spiritual Mother, over and over, and cried tears to her for her most loving and kind attention. I thought about previous messages where she had called out to the world to repent of our sins, and to stop offending the precious heart of Jesus. If I had died and gone to Heaven right then and there it would have been the only thing to equal what I felt kneeling there under a huge, full moon, on a warm August night, awaiting a visit from the Queen of Heaven.

As the last prayers were being said, my cousin and I would glance around, and then back at each other, wondering just what was going to happen. The lights had already been turned off in the church, and only candles were stationed around the outside stairway for illumination. We were told that we could use camcorders and cameras, but only ones without lights or flashbulbs. The crowd now waited quietly under the clear night sky.

A few minutes before midnight I saw a flash of light on the wall of the church. And then, at midnight, just as she had promised, flashes of light began hitting all around. Some of the lights were white, and some were brilliant colors. Some streaked across the top, and sides of the church, and some danced over and throughout the crowds. Some lights were something like those of a laser show, while others were flowing in zigzag streaks. Some were quite large like lightning charges, and some were smaller like balls of static electricity.

As several news teams, who had been following this public phenomenon for seven years, later attested, "They could see no physical sources, or logical explanations of those lights." They were very serious when they reported that they witnessed no earthly theatrics being used to create those lights that danced, and twirled and blazed through the crowd, over, throughout, and all around the church and its grounds. They could not explain what had happened.

At one point, one dazzling white light went directly between my cousin and me, and the people in front of us. I turned here and there as I watched the multitude of streams and brilliant flashes interplay with the entire crowd and church building. It was as though time had stopped while this radiant light display held me spellbound; and then, with a few faint flashes they were gone.

Father Smith thanked Our Lady for coming, and for allowing us to be a witness to her presence. I stood quietly for a while not wanting to put my thoughts into words, or my senses back into the ordinary; unwilling to move from that Hallowed setting. How do you go home after witnessing something like that, and ever be the same? I don't know how it was for everyone else that was there. I know that they all apparently witnessed the same miracle of the lights, but I do not know what they felt, or believed.

As for me, there were so many feelings that culminated in that wondrous day and night, revelations and reaffirmations of how miracles can come to us through the incidental meeting of someone in a department store, the unexpected desired prayer for a son in a desperate situation, and the welcoming news that I had been invited by the Mother of Our Lord to partake of her comforting presence, that to this day it still causes tears to run down my face when I think on it.

Because of Our Lady and her unbelievable kindness to this common and undeserving human, there is a memory in my heart of Divine love and communion, set beneath a full moon, on a miraculous summer's night, which I will relive and draw strength from forever.

CHAPTER 28

It's *Never* the last Chapter

———— ∞ ————

MOVING FORWARD TO A DAY in 2006, Jessica, Elizabeth, and Will came by my apartment to pick me up. As we were sitting at a red light, my grandson was trying to remember a dream that he had the night before. He said it was about some kind of animal.

That made me think about what I might have dreamt. Remembering, I said, "Well... of all things, I dreamt about the Crocodile Hunter." Laughing, Will asked, "Was he **wrestling** a crocodile?" I thought a little deeper. "No....he was standing waist deep in some water and there was a big white bird beside him....no, actually....it was a Sting Ray." Then we talked about the day my daughter had stepped on one in Florida that had come out from under the sand and swam off.

A short time later, after my dream, we were shocked and saddened at the tragic death of Steve Erwin, due to an encounter with a Sting Ray.

Another strange incident stands out in my mind, in 2007, when, Zackary, my grandson, was about two months old. On this certain afternoon, I lay down across my bed and fell asleep. In the dream that came, I was in a house filled with people. I caught a glimpse of my daughter, Heather, and I also saw a baby in the mixture of assorted people, although I did not know whose baby it was.

As I was standing in a crowded room, a young boy came to me and said, "Lady, that baby can't breathe." I instinctively followed as he led the way. There in the corner of the room, on some type of low to the ground carriage, was the baby I had seen earlier, and it obviously wasn't breathing.

Determining what to do, I picked it up. Its face was red, and there was foamy milk on its mouth. Its arms were rigid and straight out to the side just like a stiff baby doll as I turned it over onto my arm. I gave it four raps to the back in case it was choking on something, and then started CPR, stopping only to check for breathing. I was terrified when I realized that it wasn't responding. I again did CPR, and checked. Thank-God, that time it was breathing and appeared to be alright. (I awoke, somewhat disturbed).

A few days later, off from work, I went to visit Heather. As we sat on the couch, she exclaimed, "Oh, mom, you'll never believe what happened a few days ago." I was sitting in that chair, folding laundry, with Zackary right there beside me in his bouncy carrier. I had just looked down at him when a few seconds later I looked at him again and his face was dark red, and he wasn't breathing. I grabbed him up, and his arms were straight out and stiff, just like a plastic baby doll. I gave him mouth to mouth breaths, but he didn't respond. I was so scared to death, and frantic. I turned him over and patted his back and rubbed him all over to stimulate him, and then did some more breaths. I thought he was never going to respond. Just then, he started breathing. He cried for a moment, like he had just woken up, and then he seemed to be just fine. He had some bubbles of milk around his mouth, like he must have spit up some milk and sucked it into his windpipe as he fell asleep, or something strange like that. All I know is that I thought he was never going to take a breath. I thought he was going to die."

I told her that I had a pretty good idea of how scared and helpless she must have felt, because I appeared to have shared those agonizing moments with her in my dream.

They always say two heads are better than one; perhaps two hearts are as well.

One day, around 2006, while attending Eastern Kentucky University's RN program, the other students and I were broken up into smaller groups with a Nursing leader, who asked us to go around the circle and tell a little about ourselves.

One of the students told of the recent death of her mother, and what it meant to her and her family, and how this loss had impacted her entire life. As we went around the circle there were many stories of happiness, tragedy, and family, amongst us. I took a chance on sounding kooky, and told the group that I had written a book about the paranormal.

Several days had passed when I had the feeling of, not so much being watched, but being followed, or being "accompanied," now and then. It wasn't particularly bothersome, but as the feeling persisted I began to take a little more notice.

As the days went on, the color yellow started popping up in my mind, and it kept coming in my mind. *'Yellow, the color yellow.'* It became a very consistent sensation, and a very decisive *"yellow,"* not to be mistaken; and for some reason I started thinking, and I couldn't stop thinking, about the student in my class.

She was someone that I had never sat down and talked with, and since our initial classes were large, we may have said hi while passing in a hall, but I really did not know her at all, and yet, she was on my mind more and more as the days passed, and the color yellow felt as if it had taken on a life unto itself that would not quit following me around.

As small groups of us were sitting in the hall one day, each awaiting our turn to demonstrate our blood pressure skills, Jenny walked up to me because of what I had said about the book I had written. A little shy at first, she said, "I believe in ghosts, and things like that. My boyfriend and I just stayed in a motel that had all kinds of noises in it. The people around the town said that it was haunted. I have always believed in things like that." A couple of other students nodded in agreement, and said that they believed in ghosts, too.

Not long after this, I was in a gift shop/restaurant, with my daughter, when that feeling of someone standing close to me, and walking with me, came on very strongly. "Yellow, tell her yellow. Tell her yellow," it persisted.

Don't ask me how, but right then, I just knew that the person that I must talk to about this was the young woman who had lost her mother..... and I was pretty sure that I had found her, or should I say, she found me.

I felt the desire to buy a small present for Jenny, and I chose a small one, one of faith and remembrance, that one can carry around. I had it gift wrapped, and I gave it to her the next day, telling her that I was so sorry to hear about the loss of her mother.

Being shy myself, it took me a while to get up my nerve to approach Jenny on the subject that seemed to now be following me everywhere I went, with strong conviction of "yellow." Not thinking of myself as a psychic, and still don't, I sat down beside her one day, alone, on some bleachers.

"I know that you don't really know me, and I wouldn't want to upset you, or anything, but I just have to talk to you. I asked her, "Does the color yellow mean anything to you? Is there something about your mother and the color yellow?" Jenny's eyes widened, and she looked very stunned, but then answered, "Yes...... *she* was!" She explained further, "I know it may sound morbid, but she was so jaundiced by the time that she got really sick, and to make it seem less sad, my sister and I had would kid her, and say, "Mom you are so yellow," and she always laughed along with us."

Mom said that when she passed, she would find someone, some way, to let us know that she was alright, and was with us".

"I have goosebumps," I said, rubbing my arms, and Jenny said that she did too, knowing that I had no way of knowing this information about her, and the condition of her mother.

We sat quietly for a moment, taking it in. Jenny said that she really believed that her mother did send that message to her, and that she was still with her and her family. And, I do too. As odd a message as that was, it is this kind of personal, random validation that truly makes us find comfort and inspiration in our sometimes lonely walk.

The stories that I have included in my book started somewhere around 1965, and it is now 2017, and as I come around to what feels like a full circle, to the here and present, I will leave you with three of my most recent accounts, the first, starting with activities occurring in the house that my daughter, Heather, moved into when she married in 2005. The house was only a few years old at this time, and her husband, who was already living there, was its first owner.

Everything about the house seemed very normal, and in 2007, their first child, Zackary, was born. Because this was my daughter's first child, and the newly furnished nursery was upstairs, and quite a distance, Zackary slept downstairs in their bedroom.

However, sometimes Heather would take the baby upstairs to the nursery to feed and rock him in her new brown chair, and it didn't take long before she started noticing that she never felt quite comfortable in that room, and often would feel as though she were being watched from the closet. Sometimes the hair on the back of her neck would stand up, and she seriously wondered if she opened the closet, would someone be in there, looking at her. But, Heather kept this to herself.

Heather and her husband rarely went out without Zackary, but when they did, on a few occasions, I would come over to be with him, and several times I spent the night. The first night that I stayed over, alone with Zackary, he was about two years old. We had a wonderful day of laughing and playing together, and then came bedtime.

I got Zackary ready for bed, and then we lay down in the bedroom downstairs. I was listening to his baby talk and laughter, and thinking how cute he was, when he sat up in bed, and very seriously looked past me, and up to the ceiling. He appeared to be looking at, or watching something very real, and seemed very captivated. For a moment, I recalled the feeling of fear that I had felt at Wolfe Pen, when my little daughter would appear to be seeing frightful things that I could not see.

Zackary lay back down and I tried to continue with innocent fun and talk, but after a moment or so he sat up again, looking past me, and started studying the ceiling again. This time, I too had the hair stand up on my arms and the back of my neck. I hate to admit it, but when he would go from smiles to frowns as he watched intently, that old icy feeling went up my spine. Not wanting to believe it, I was absolutely sure that that he was watching something, or somebody.

I felt very scared, and I felt angry, because it wasn't fair. I knew that this baby was being shown something that was there, but adults couldn't see it. The same behavior happened exactly the same, one other time as I stayed alone with him. I started saying prayers.

In 2009, Luke was born. A few months later, I had spent a wonderful day taking care of the boys. While Luke slept in his bassinette, beside the bed, Zackary and I got ready to go to sleep. Everything felt relaxed and comfortable. He was happy, and I was happy. And then, he sat straight up, looked over and past me, and started watching the ceiling again.

Once again, he would go between smiles and frowns, while staring intently. But when he made a face, and crossly said "**No**," to whatever was up there, it made my skin crawl. What had been said? What had been asked of him?

I understand that to some people this would be easily dismissed, slightly odd behavior of a toddler. And in some other life, and on some other planet, to me, it might be as well. However, not having chosen for my little girl, Jessica, and myself, to be attacked and stalked by an unseen entity, or entities, it was very unnerving. To me it rang of sneakiness and ugliness.

I had told my daughter about the occurrences with Zackary, but we just sort of put them away in some little corner of our minds, and tried not to dwell on it. However, she had not been telling me of the odd nursery uneasiness and apprehension that she had felt, or that had seemed to be escalating, now that Luke was sleeping in his crib upstairs.

Starting in 2009, when he was around eight months old, Luke would often climb the stairs by himself, to play with the toys in the nursery, and because he loved to take naps, he would also climb into bed. Heather had already taken the sides off of his crib, which turned it into a low, day bed, making it easier for him to climb in and out. But more and more often, when she checked on him, she was finding him asleep behind the big brown rocker. She took a slight note that it was the farthest corner away from the closet, and to her, that closet still felt strange.

When Luke was around one year old, he started having night terrors, and his screaming would send her flying upstairs. She said that it reminded her of her sister, Jessica, who had suffered from night terrors that started at Wolfe Pen, and happened frequently until well into her twenties. (She still occasionally has some night terrors, but thank God, mostly they have subsided).

For a while it was as though the episodes had quieted down, but as in so many cases, they came back with a vengeance. One afternoon, very typically, Luke had gotten sleepy, and had crawled up the stairs. All at once, Heather heard such blood curdling screams coming from him that it sounded as though he were being physically attacked. She said she believed she had taken three steps at a time to get to him, that's how horrific his screams were.

When she ran into the nursery, Luke was on the floor, on his stomach, screaming and crying, in an unnatural position that looked as if he were being dragged under the bed. His legs and abdomen were all the way under, and he was digging his hands and fingers into the carpet, as if trying to keep from being pulled in further. (We're talking about a baby that is less than two years old.)

Heather felt very uneasy, and so disturbed by the whole experience that she moved the brown rocker down to the living room, and from then on Zackary and Luke slept downstairs with her, and her husband. For the next five or so years, the nursery was off limits, and the door stayed closed. My daughter only went in now and then to get clothing from the chest and closet. It always felt eerie to her, and life seemed to be slightly 'out of the ordinary.'

In between the last of my episode with Zachary and the ceiling, when he was still a small toddler, something very disturbing happened while Heather, and Zackery, and Luke were the only ones in her house.

One evening, Zackary was sitting at the kitchen table, with one leg under the other, deeply engrossed in coloring his book, when Heather saw her camera on the kitchen counter, and decided that she should put it in the dining room, out of the way. She picked it up, walked to the dining room, which was about six or so feet away, laid it down, turned right around and walked back into the kitchen. She stopped point blank, and stifled a scream.

You may remember the scene in the Sixth Sense, **5** when the mother walked into one room, turned around, and walked back, and every cabinet door was open. Only in Heather's case, it wasn't cabinet doors, the other three chairs around the kitchen table were lying on their backs on the floor, and were perfectly, uniformly lined around the table's curve. Zackary was still sitting in his chair, still intent on his coloring book, still sitting in the same position, with the same leg under him.

Shaken, and baffled by the bizarre display of the chairs, which are very tall, and very heavy, she asked Zackary what happened to the chairs. He looked up at her, but didn't seem to know what she was talking about. She showed him the chairs, but he didn't have any particular interest in them. Anyway, she knew in her heart, that he didn't put those chairs in the floor, and couldn't have, if he tried.

She later asked him to lay a chair down for her, but he was not able to hold onto it long enough to place it on the floor. It was too heavy. Her husband, who had been at work, thought that Zackary must have done it, but when he tried himself to recreate the pattern, he got them all on the floor, but it took quite a few minutes, and it made a lot of noise. He wasn't able to simulate it.

Heather knew that it was not possible for Zackary to do that, either. It was just too supernaturally quiet, and fast, and impossible for the only person in the room, a little boy, less than three years old.

I know firsthand, that it is always frightening, and very perplexing when something so out of the ordinary happens, especially in your own home, that it gives you a worry, and uneasiness, because you cannot see, nor would you want to, who, or whatever it is that is invading your space.

I will add a third, and final incident that happened while just the boys and I were in the house. It was after my daughter had finally told me all about Luke and the nursery room experiences, and also after the night of the kitchen chairs, when, she was so shaken, she had immediately called me. Trust me, by then I already had the same uneasiness about this house that she did.

One day when Zackary was three, and Luke was two, while Heather and Scott were out, I had spent the day playing with the two boys. Luke fell asleep watching cartoons, and I told Zackary that we should also take a nap for a little while.

He happily walked in front of me through the living room, and went to the bed. I wasn't planning on taking a nap, but just wanted to rest. It was just a few moments after we got settled down, when Zackary sat up, looked up to the ceiling, and started smiling, as if being in on a funny game, and announced, "Here they come....gh-gh-gh-ghosts!" (Trust me, I wasn't smiling.)

He sat there for just a moment longer, captivated by something around the ceiling, and then he lay down. (I guess the show was over). I definitely wasn't in the mood for a nap, now, and I really felt quite unnerved by all of these episodes, although I didn't let on to Zackary.

After we rested, Zackary followed as I walked back into the living room. Something caught my eye, in the middle of the floor, and I stopped to look over. There, not but a few feet from where we had walked when we went to lie down, were four or five of his Thomas the Engine cars, lined up, and standing on end.

They looked so odd. How had I missed them, if they had been lined up in that odd formation, when we had first walked through the living room? Wondering, and waiting for Zackary's reaction, if any, I watched him as he caught up, and then he stopped and looked over at them. I could tell by the look on his face as he studied them that it wasn't something that he had seen before.

He stood there and looked quite curiously surprised at the train cars standing on end, and in a perfect line, and then he broke out into a smile, as if so delighted and amazed that someone had put them that way. To this day, I still wonder how they were able to balance on end, anyway, but I didn't walk over and look.

Sometimes it seems easier to just put things away in some part of your mind, and not wonder or worry so much about it. But in my life, and my family and friends, as in so many cases, maybe we really don't want to know, but it just never seems to be left that way.

Not long after, when Heather and her husband and the boys carved pumpkins that year, she lined them all on her kitchen table to take pictures. Every picture was taken in just a few seconds difference of the others, however, in one there is a bright light streak that goes across one of the pictures. When she showed me the pictures a few days later of how cute the pumpkins looked, when I saw the light streak, I remarked, "*Well,* **there's** your ghost."

Things seem to quieten down for the next two years or so, and having birthday parties for the boys were always something fun and special, and always meant balloons. Almost always, at least one balloon would escape and hang around in the twenty foot ceiling that opened over the living room and upstairs play area.

Heather and the boys would always watch it, and try to guess when the escapee balloon would deflate and come down. Not too much time would pass, and the balloons would run out of helium, and feather down.

The year that Zackary turned five, in 2012, the same thing happened, only this time, this balloon was different. As the many days passed, and then the many weeks passed, this balloon stayed high and full. One evening, when just Heather and the boys were at home, the balloon, which was high over the living room, started spinning, and then swiftly took off across the ceiling, and ended up in the playroom area, just outside of the nursery door. The door that still stayed closed.

Heather felt a little puzzled at how, and why it had acted so oddly. Now that the balloon was in that part of the upstairs, the string could be reached, and she sent Zackary up to catch it while it was in the play area. When he brought it down to her, Heather then released it, and it floated back up to the high living room ceiling.

But, of course, that wasn't the end of it. Only a few minutes had passed when the balloon again started wildly spinning. "Look at the balloon, Zack," she exclaimed. And then, it sped off, as though being pulled by its string across the ceiling, and ending up outside of the nursery door, once again. With phone already in hand, she was able to film almost the entire incident.

It was rather strange, and more than peculiar, given all of the other incidents that had been happening in the house, and to the children. The air vents are low throughout the house, and there wasn't any kind of draft going on up there. She knew this, because the curtains that are over the second story part of the living room, close to where the balloon hung out, were not moving at all. There wasn't an air flow, or vent in the area. The balloon sailed across the ceiling, and toward the nursery, as though being pulled by an invisible hand.

They left the balloon where it was. The next morning, still on her mind, she didn't see it in any of the usual spots. She went upstairs. It wasn't a pleasant surprise when she looked over to find that the nursery door was open, and the balloon was inside, up on the ceiling. How did that balloon go low enough to get under the doorway, and then back up to the ceiling in that room? And Heather did not want to even think about why that door was open, or why the balloon seemed determined to get into the nursery. It was getting to be too much.

Due to the immersion, and unwilling participation of so many strange activities that have invaded our lives, my immediate family has known about burning sage, and fanning it throughout houses and areas that have been haunted, or had suspicious paranormal activity. And it was no surprise to me that a few months later when my granddaughter went to visit her aunt, Heather, that they saged the entire house, especially the closet and crawl space in the Nursery.

Since then, I am relieved to say that there have not been any more noteworthy, or scary episodes. But am I holding my breath? Maybe.

My second account, which finishes my Eastern Kentucky College experience, is concerning the apartment/house that I lived in while attending school.

I decided that I should get an apartment of my own in the campus housing in Richmond. As soon as I applied, the woman in student housing said that she had something available, and that it might be just what I needed. After looking over the efficiency apartment, which consisted of a large living room, a small bathroom, and a good-sized kitchen, I happily accepted.

It was the bottom floor of an old three story house, and all of the doors and windows and features in the house were big, and open, and let in a lot of light. It was charming and quaint, and even though my bathroom and half of my kitchen went underground as a basement, my front, and only door, was full of glass panels, and my living room and kitchen windows were large, too, and opened onto an almost country setting sidewalk, even though it was right in the middle of the city.

Is was not long after settling in, when I had an odd dream. In the dream, I was standing by one of my living room windows, along with some unidentified people. "Someone hung themselves," I said. And that was the end of my dream.

It didn't take long to meet my other house mates. They all worked for the college, in different maintenance fields, and were very friendly.

Millie lived on what we called the third floor, and Tom and his three boys lived on the second floor, right above me, and Bill lived in the apartment behind me, on the same level as mine, his being totally above ground, though.

I soon became good friends with all of them, especially Bill, and after I had lived there for a few weeks, he asked me how I liked my apartment. I noticed that he sort of looked like he half expected me to say that I didn't. "Oh, I love it," I answered. "It feels so homey and comfortable." Again I sensed that he had something to say. "What?" I asked. "Is there something wrong?" "No, no," he said," "I......I was just wondering." "What is it?" I asked, because I could tell that he wanted to say more."

"Are you afraid of ghosts?" he asked, hesitantly. "Heck, yes," I felt like saying, but didn't. Instead, I said that I believed in ghosts, and wanted to know why he was asking. Bill told me that a young maintenance man had hung himself in that apartment, a couple of years before, over a broken relationship. He added that they hadn't found him for several days.

"Oh," I said. "That is so sad. Come to think of it, I had a dream that someone had hung themselves." It turned out that it was from one of the large pipes that ran the length of my living room ceiling, close to my window, the window in my dream.

When I went in that night, I have to admit that I was a little apprehensive, after what all had happened in the past, and I hoped that I wouldn't feel differently about my little home. But in all of the years that I lived there, I never felt scared of the young man, or my apartment, and I sent up many little encouraging prayers in hopes that he was happy and found peace.

Tom, my upstairs neighbor, continued to get up and loudly clomp around over my head every morning at 4:30, but life was pretty simple and stress free during those years. Often, I would watch him and the boys get their fishing gear ready for evening or weekend outings, and some-times Bill would go with them.

Otherwise, occasionally, Bill and I would sit in the backyard and pass the time. One night, he asked me if I had heard all the loud footsteps over the weekend. I told him that I did, and that Tom must wear some heavy work shoes. "Did he have to work this weekend?" I asked. Bill gave me a glance, and confided, "Tom and his boys were gone all weekend.... there wasn't anybody at home."

I was trying to figure out if Bill was saying that we had been visited by a burglar, or what. He kind of grinned, and asked, "Haven't you been hear-ing those loud footsteps, early in the morning?" "Yes," I answered. "Are you telling me that Tom or his boys aren't making any of those noises?" "No, it's not Tom," Bill replied," then he added, "I guess you haven't had the knocking on your door, yet, either?"

After EKU had bought the house to use as student housing, through the years, evidently, as the story goes, several tenants had seen an elderly lady in the upstairs apartment, a ghostly apparition walking through the house. What's more, many a tenant had gone to answer knocks on their doors, during the day or night, only to find that no one was there. They had all been caught at one time another, standing perplexed at an empty doorway.

The loud thumps and stomping continued every morning, and one night, a crash so loud, caused me to jerk my head to the ceiling, along with my dog. It sounded as though something very heavy had fallen onto a wooden floor. Later I asked Tom if something had fallen that night, and shook the floor. He didn't know of anything like that happening, at all.

It all really surprised me, especially after Tom moved, for when Bill and I went into Tom's bedroom, where all of the footsteps had taken place, and the spot where the loud commotion had jarred me, to find that his bedroom was carpeted. It wasn't bare flooring as I had imagined. And the area that was over my living room corresponded with part of his bed-room, and part of his bathroom. There wasn't room for anyone to walk around in that area because of the wall, even if someone had tried.

At times, I could be walking in my apartment, and a resounding thud would hit behind me on the old wooden floor boards. I always assumed that the wood was somehow bending and or flexing with pressure. It wasn't scary, but it was definitely odd. Looking back, I don't believe that those floors could naturally cause that sound, or create the physical thud ripple. But if it were the young maintenance man, or the phenomenon of residual energy, often left by traumatic events, it just didn't scare me. Don't ask me why not, because I don't know, and I'm not that brave, either.

The only time that I actually did feel uncomfortable, or wary, though, was when Millie moved out of the third floor. It was the night that I walked into my bathroom, and I had an eerie, unshakable feeling that I was being watched. It was very hard to stay in there because it was so physical. For three days I could barely make myself take a shower, or go in to change my clothes, or attend to my business. Someone's eyes were just burning into me every time I walked in there.

I examined the walls carefully, in case someone had actually created a peep hole, and was looking at me while I was inside my bathroom, from outside, or from inside the basement. But there was nothing like that to be found, and it didn't matter if it were at day break, or afternoon, or the middle of the night, those invisible eyes were always there. For three days. But after the third day, it was gone. Completely and utterly gone. Not a trace, not an inkling, not a bit of sensation left, and I never did have that feeling again.

The final odd thing that happened while I was in that apartment, was when I was asleep on my couch, and someone persistently knocking at my door woke me up. As I fumbled around in the semi-dark, my eyes met the clock, it was 4:30 in the morning. The rapping continued as I quietly walked to the door. Without having a phone, I was very vulnerable. "Oh, no," I thought. "Something must be wrong, or my daughter would not be coming this early in the morning." But, then, I also considered that a stranger might have wandered down my sidewalk, and was trying to get in. There were a couple of bars only a few blocks down in the city, and everyone knew that this was student housing.

The constant rapping had stopped just as I approached the door. Before opening it, I peered out of my right window, to the street where my daughter always parked when she visited, but the street was empty. I then peeped out of the curtain that covered my glass paneled door. No one was there. As I always kept one window fixed opened six or so inches, I listened for the sound of footsteps, or any out of the way noises, or any sign that someone was outside….but there was nothing.

To make myself feel better and be assured that all was well, I decided to open my door and check it out. Remembering what I had been told about the house, I crossed myself, and then said out loud, "You are not welcome to come in here, and I do not want you to come in, in Jesus' name." With that, I opened my door, and looked all around my yard and street. All was quiet and peaceful.

It remained that way, nothing else out of the ordinary happened again, and when I moved back to Louisville, to my childhood home, to help take care of my mom, I took only memories, albeit strange ones, at that.

My final story is about my mother who passed away on the last day of March, 2016, while I was lying next to her in the hospital. In the pre-dawn, while still holding onto her arm, as I had all through the night, I was ever so gently and brokenheartedly aware when she took her last breath.

I was an adult, and we had seen many ups and downs in our relationship, before, and during the years that I had come home to take care of her needs and keep her company. I had dealt with death many times as a Caregiver, personally, and with mom being so elderly and sick, I had been preparing myself for some time, that she would be leaving me.

But, I did not know how hard that this would hit me, and the depth of sadness and pain that would overcome me at every opportunity of the day, and especially at night. Touching her clothing, looking at her pictures, seeing the little touches that she had made in this home were almost unbearable. Because, in the end, you only have one mommy.

I cherished the moments that I held close in my heart, but now those memories were as painful and cutting, as they were kind and comforting. Now, it is only me, living in the house that my father had physically built, overwhelmed with so many years of memories and emotions, it causes me to wonder whether I am happy, or sad because of it.

As it always does, time passes, but not the hurt, or the sense of loss. I had started using my old bedroom again, when mom died, and it was the room that she had slept in as she had gotten older. I kept using the pretty glass night light that she had used toward the last few years.

One early morning, after a particularly sad night, I had just turned over, when I sensed that the night light went out. I lay there, pondering whether I had forgotten to pay the electric bill, but, no, I definitely had, and my fan was still humming away. I lay there for a minute or two. "Well, I thought to myself, I guess the bulb finally burnt out." I had no more than thought this, when the light came back on. It wasn't a flicker, it definitely had been off, and now it was back on.

No big deal, I thought, sometimes things just happen. A few days later, once again in the wee hours, I had woken up, and was lying still, when I sensed that the light went off again. "I guess the bulb finally did burn out this time," I thought to myself. I lay there, resting quietly, when the light came back on. I thought about mom this time, but didn't dwell on it.

The next day I checked the light itself, and made sure that the bulb was tight, and everything was in order. Lights can flicker, but this wasn't a flickering thing. It was going off, and waiting before it came back on again. Up to this point, I really didn't know what to think. When it did it again, I knew what to think.

It was early one morning, predawn, and I had just woke up and realized that the moon was quite full, because I could see it shining around my window shade. I pulled the shade up, and lay down on the end of my bed so that I could look at it, and the lit street and yards, the way I had when I was growing up. The light went out again, and this time, I did think of mom. I was hoping that it was her, and that she was okay and happy, and maybe just letting me know that she was near. And, just like that, the light came back on, and now, months later, it has never done that since. Not even one little flicker. In fact, it was ten months later when I actually had to change the bulb.

Time passed, and little changed with my sadness. I had my good days, and my bad days, but I couldn't seem to think about any happy days except those in the past, and I felt like life had slipped by, and had taken all of those wonderful people in my life with it, and that each day could be another goodbye to someone else. I was going through depression.

We might know in our hearts that love never dies, and that there is hope and beauty and joy at the end when we are all reunited, but it does not spare us, nor does it mean to, the grief and sense of loss, the utter sadness and loneliness that we are sometimes so ill equipped to deal with.

Grief is not kind, by any means, and I feel much sadness for those who are in situations where they are totally cut off from the support of loved ones and friends. But please remember, the outside world may not be able to reach you, but God can, and the loved ones waiting on the other side can. That is the reason that I am telling these accounts, for anyone who will believe, to take some hope and comfort from them.

A short time ago, as I sat at my computer, late one night, the bulb at the bottom of the stairs exploded into miniature fragments, causing the plastic shade to drop along with them. It startled me, and caused a moment of alarm, in case there would be an electrical issue following. I quickly ran up the stairs and turned off the switch. Eyeing the damage, I saw that all of the glass pieces had fallen neatly in a little pile.

Thinking back on the nights that we had watched different shows about mediums, and knowing that it really would be hard for her to see me so distressed and sad, night after night, I half-jokingly asked, "Mom, is that you?"

I sat back down and started to write again, when little musical notes started playing, slowly at first, and then in perfect time. I looked around to see where it was coming from, and my eyes stopped on a music box that was sitting on a shelf of the bookcase that my dad had built.

I listened until it played itself out, quite a little moment, and then it abruptly stopped. Half whispering, half hoping, half smiling, I asked once again, "Mom, is that you, are you here with me?"

After a year had passed, and after careful consideration of my financial outlook, and my ability to work less hours per week, I decided to sell the family home. I had decided on a plan that would give me a smaller home, and provide a little more income coming in, whether I was working or not.

With much deliberation, I felt that I was doing the right thing. It was a good plan, but it didn't relieve me of the pain and sadness of yet another familiar loss. After all, my dad had physically built that house, and my mom had taken care of it for over 67 years. My brother and I had spent many years there.

It did not take me long at all to find the condo that I wanted to live in. The minute that I stepped into the living room, and on throughout the rooms, I knew that it was the one. I had only seen a few other condos, but I loved it, and knowing how quickly two other condos had just sold, I told my real estate agent that I wanted to put in an offer.

A contract was written out and sent on to the other agent, and in just twenty-four hours, I was bound to a condo that I had barely seen, and only for a short time. That night I could not sleep. I became very anxious, and feared that I had perhaps made a big mistake by acting too quickly. Maybe I didn't really know what I was doing, and that I had been foolish, acting in a very careless and impulsive way. I tossed and I turned, and I worried, like I had never worried before.

When I got up the next morning, I really didn't feel any better about my hasty decision. I did love the condo, at least I thought I did, but when I started gathering boxes, and packing up the precious pictures and keepsakes that once belonged to my mother and father, I became very sad, and very anxious about the decision that I had just made.

To keep me motivated, I turned on the radio in the kitchen. It was tuned to an oldie country music station. As I sat in the chair, the pain of missing my mom, and also my dad, hurt so much, and I wished that life could just be simple again. I wished that I knew for certain that I was making the right decisions, and choosing the right property.

Suddenly the song on the radio switched to a totally different song, and a totally different type of music. *"If you want it, here it is, come and get it, but you better hurry or it may not last.... you better hurry cause it's going fast."*4

I knew that song so well. It was an oldie rock and roll song. But the words, I couldn't believe the words! It was as though my mom and dad were telling me to go for it. Buy the condo that you love, and be happy with your decision. And you needn't waste time looking and second guessing yourself, when the one you want is right here, right now.

I know that it may sound silly or irrational to some of you, but to me it was the words that I so desperately needed from my parents. I walked over to the radio, and I literally had to turn the knob back around to get the station that I started out with. It hadn't faded in and out. It had physically jumped from one station to the other.

When I moved into my own condo a weeks ago, I asked my mom and dad to please come with me, and any of my loved ones. And just to be safe, I also prayed, and adamantly stated that no uninvited visitors, or past residents of any kind were allowed here. Period.

As I began unpacking and getting my home set up, I tried to make a macramé hanger for a plant, out of thin rope. After several attempts, with odd lengths of rope, I laid it all on the floor, and left the pieces here and there. I had a lot of boxes to unpack.

I had mostly been sitting on a certain end of the couch, day after day, night after night, while I watched television, or talked on the phone, which was close by. I had crossed the living room many times, going in and out, and throughout the house.

One afternoon, after a particularly sad night of missing my mom, as I was talking to my son on the phone, something caught my eye, not more than four feet in front of me, on the carpet. It was a piece of the rope that I had used, and left on the floor. But, how had I missed this? The rope was in a perfect cursive H.

My mother's name is Hazel, and I have so many pieces of jewelry, and zipper clasps, charms, and anything that can be made into an initial, with the letter H, just like it. I really don't know how I could have missed it, sitting there, day after day; and how did it fall to the carpet and make such a perfect H?

And to be honest, actually....I don't think that the rope just fell that way, and that somehow I overlooked it. I think that it was arranged there by my mom. We had our differences throughout our relationship, but in my mind, I can still hear her say, just like she used to, "Don't cry, Diane, I love you."

After being back in the childhood home, and being back with mom those last nine years, it has been particularly hard since her death, and I have cried a lot, and I still do. Watching your mother suffer for years, and then watching her die, is the kind of experience that is traumatic, to say the least, and it leaves a disquieted memory, and a wounded, empty space in your heart.

As mom had gotten older, she and I would watch shows about such things as mediums, and the afterlife. She knew that I was already a believer, and I think she wanted some assurance for herself that life goes on, and that there is something greater than us out there, and that it is not the end. I am not surprised that she would get my attention in whatever way she could, to let me know that she found the answer that she was looking for.

Yes, I still have dreams about things that have either happened while I was sleeping, or came about in the future; and out-of-the-blue premonitions and warnings still tug at me fairly regularly, along with all of the past occurrences that I didn't include in this book. I have delivered, with much prayer and deliberation, more messages from those that have passed on, to a few of their selected loved ones, and I do greatly wonder about these things that have happened in my life.

I would like to say, and let me be really straightforward about this, I do not believe that we should carelessly seek out what is not seen, or fully understood. To me, the activity and reason of that which we cannot fully comprehend, or those who may or may not be under God's sanctity are not to be played with. This earthly life has enough activities, miracles and personalities to keep us entertained for a lifetime, and what we don't know, or that which is hidden, is usually that way for a good reason. I would whole heartily suggest that you don't naively invite in, or seek out the spirit world, and NEVER, under any circumstances, use a Ouija board.

I still marvel at those things that are odd or perplexing, including all of the bad choices and mistakes that I have made....but not as much as I used to.

"Relax, laugh, do!" I try to remind myself. Do what you can today; be the best that you can be with as little pain to yourself and others as possible. Allow yourself to be happy (this should involve no pain whatsoever). Reach out blindly for God, and take a giant leap of faith toward life. You're going to land one way or another, so aim for something soft; something decent and kind. That has always been your choice; it has always been in your hands.

Then leave the rest up to God.

Paul and Hazel Satterfield, my mom and dad,
when they were in their twenties.

A very neatly shattered light bulb

The picture perfect Cursive H

Christopher, Jessica, and Heather (and me)

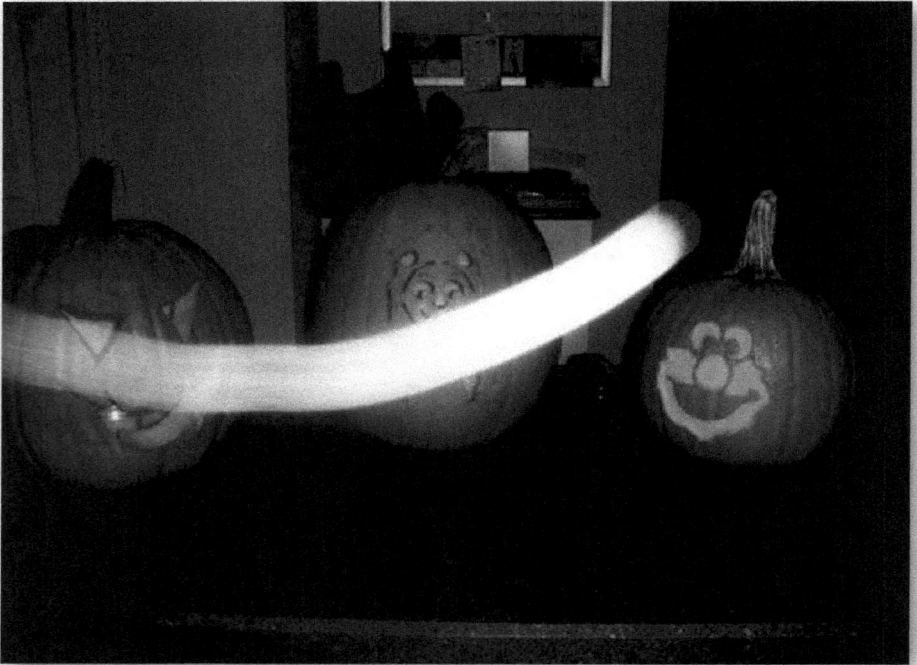

Of the four in a row photos that Heather took of the pumpkins, only
the third one had this strange streak of light going across it.

APPENDIX

WITH THE EXCEPTION OF MY immediate family, the names of most people in my accounts have been changed to protect their privacy.

WORKS CITED

1. Silbar J. and Henley L. 1982 "Wind beneath my wings." Beaches. Perf. by Bette Midler. USA, 1988. Film.

2. Fain S. and Kahal I. 1938 "I'll be seeing you." Perf. by Billie Holliday. https://youtu.be/zDlKb2cBAqU

3. Gibran, Kahlil. The Prophet. 1st ed. Vol. 1. USA: Alfred A. Knopf, 1923.

4. M. Night Shyamalan. Screenplay and Director. The Sixth Sense. Perf. by Bruce Willis and Haley Joel Osment. USA: Spyglass Entertainment, 1999. Film.

5. Paul McCartney. "Come and Get It." 24 July 1969 England. Apple records.

AUTHOR'S NOTES

—⊗⊗⊗—

DIANE SATTERFIELD WAS BORN IN Louisville, Kentucky, where she still resides. Her ancestry is that of Appalachian coal miners from Tennessee and Eastern Kentucky, and Southern Indiana farmers. She is very proud of the good natured humor and close bonds in those family traditions, and of the hard work and creative skills that were deeply rooted into this critical and common sense blended heritage.

The last two summers she has hosted a Paranormal Appalachian workshop for the Whippoorwill Festival, in Eastern Kentucky, where everyone was welcomed to tell their own unique stories, and discuss the paranormal aspects of life.

The sketch on the back page is one that Ms. Satterfield drew of the Angelic cloud.

www.ingramcontent.com/pod-product-compliance
Lightning Source LLC
Chambersburg PA
CBHW061432040426
42450CB00007B/1014